The Practical Guide
to Transforming
Your Company

The Practical Guide to Transforming Your Company

Daniel L. Plung
Connie J. Krull

BEP BUSINESS EXPERT PRESS

The Practical Guide to Transforming Your Company
Copyright © Business Expert Press, LLC, 2020.

First published in 2020 by
Business Expert Press, LLC
222 East 46th Street, New York, NY 10017
www.businessexpertpress.com

ISBN-13: 978-1-95152-744-0 (paperback)
ISBN-13: 978-1-95152-745-7 (e-book)

Business Expert Press Supply and Operations Management Collection

Collection ISSN: 2156-8189 (print)
Collection ISSN: 2156-8200 (electronic)

Cover image licensed by Ingram Image, StockPhotoSecrets.com
Cover and interior design by S4Carlisle Publishing Services Private Ltd., Chennai, India

First edition: 2020

10 9 8 7 6 5 4 3 2 1

Printed in the United States of America.

Abstract

The Practical Guide to Transforming Your Company is a concise handbook for conducting business transformations—defining and implementing a redirection in the company's core business or in its strategic positioning. Starting where such programs as LEAN and Six Sigma leave off, this text is focused on providing a successfully demonstrated methodology for conducting a comprehensive transformation (not a process-by-process efficiency enhancement).

The book lays out a well-proven methodology examining the process in detail—from determining whether a transformation is needed, to conducting the transformation, to transitioning into the new company environment. Designed as an easy-to-follow narrative, the book highlights several government and commercial projects from the United States, Canada, and the United Kingdom to help illuminate key success factors and explains the process using dozens of forms, figures, templates, and checklists the authors have developed through personal experience leading successful transformations. Enhancing the book's practical orientation, individual chapters are devoted to the roles and responsibilities of the company leadership, the workforce, and the board of directors.

Written by two individuals with extensive senior strategic management experience, this book represents the distillation of several decades of real-world experience and is bound to produce success in any transformation endeavor.

Keywords

transformation; strategic planning; corporate restructuring; market disruption; productivity enhancement; reinvention; enterprise restructuring

Contents

Acknowledgments

We thank Vickie, Nathan, and Dylan for their encouragement and support. In addition, we thank Benson for his invaluable contributions of time, expertise, and insights. Lastly, we thank Dr. Peter Kures, without whose talent and capabilities this book would never have been written.

Introduction:
The Three Predicates of Our Transformation Model

The Battle of Lepanto in 1571 changed the world—not just in turning back the Ottoman Empire's growing expansion into the Mediterranean and in securing the defense of Europe, but also in defining what may be the first true transformation of an industry. The defeat of the Ottoman navy by the Holy League's 206 galleys was largely a function of having transformed the shipbuilding industry at the Arsenal at Venice.

In the fifteenth and sixteenth centuries, the Arsenal, the "House of Manufacture," at Venice transformed centuries-old shipbuilding production methods—sequencing construction activities to create production lines manned by teams of specialists; standardizing and prefabricating major ship segments and galley designs; producing interchangeable ship features; warehousing and staging interrelated components of the ship; and ensuring production crews were supplied with a timely and uninterrupted flow of parts and materials. Complementing these production innovations, the Arsenal introduced rigorous accounting practices, robust quality controls, and formal administration of deliveries and raw materials. The success—for the shipyard and for those who relied on the Arsenal's galleys in war—was not achieved by overhauling one or two processes, but, rather, represented the comprehensive re-evaluation, restructuring, and re-integration of all facets of the operation—business, administration, planning, production, and strategic vision.

This one illustration of a major innovation that changed the course of history underscores our three predicates of conducting effective industry transformations that shape the methodology detailed in this book:

Predicate 1: *Industry disruptions are part of the contemporary marketplace. The key is being ready to transform when opportunity knocks.*

Predicate 2: *To continue to prosper, industry must step beyond the current focus on repairing and streamlining business on a process-by-process basis.*

Predicate 3: *Transformation requires a readily implementable methodology tailored to the company's strategic goals and that does not, during the process of the transformation, interrupt ongoing operations or business functions.*

As a prelude to detailing our transformation methodology, it will be beneficial briefly to examine each of these predicates to articulate how, within the lengthy evolution of the productivity movement, our methodology represents the logical synergy of and successor to contemporary process improvement methodologies such as LEAN and Six Sigma.

Predicate 1: Opportunity for Innovation/Industry Disruptions Abounds

As with the Arsenal at Venice, throughout history there have been events and innovations that have precipitated major societal shifts—shifts in how we conduct business, fight our wars, live our daily lives, and communicate with one another. Considering a small sample of influential innovations—some better known than others—distributed across a broad span of continents and time will assist in informing our first predicate: Opportunities to create market differentiation, enhance business performance, and achieve corporate redefinition (essentially openings to disrupt industries) have and will always exist:

1. In 1440 Mainz, Germany, Johannes Gutenberg's printing press helped spur on the Renaissance; his introduction of movable type revolutionized literacy, democratized information, hastened the decline of Latin, and assisted in standardizing language, grammar, and spelling.

2. Having discovered that faraway objects looked closer when viewed through two lenses, in 1608, Hans Lippershey, a Dutch spectacle maker, created the telescope. Initially referred to by him as a "looker,"

the telescope ultimately stretched man's vision and deepened our understanding of the universe.

3. Thomas Newcomen, a century later, gave us one of the major driving forces fueling the Industrial Revolution. In 1710, committed to solving the problem of removing water that flooded local mines as they became progressively deeper, Newcomen designed and built a reciprocating steam engine. Within a few years of their first use, these engines were in use throughout England and Europe.

4. Forty years after the first constant electric light was demonstrated in 1835, Thomas Edison produced both a more durable filament and a more effective means of creating the vacuum within the bulb. Further, he secured his invention's permanence by inventing the "Edison screw" (the standard socket fittings for light bulbs still in use today).

5. Although best known for invention of the cotton gin, Eli Whitney had a profound impact on modern manufacturing—demonstrating the efficiency and production flexibility resulting from use of interchangeable parts. Working on a government contract to produce rifles, he made each of the various parts of the rifle (such as stocks and triggers) exactly the same, simplifying assembly.

6. In 1876, approximately a half century after the telegraph was invented, Alexander Graham Bell publicly demonstrated the telephone using wires between two telegraph offices to transmit voices. Although given the chance to buy Bell's patent, Western Union declined because they considered it a novelty.

7. Not many years later, the Wright Brothers' 1903 adventure at Kitty Hawk introduced manned flight. Having introduced wing warping coupled with a movable rudder, the Wright brothers flew the first successful flight of a power-driven, heavier-than-air plane—on the fourth flight of the day staying aloft for 59 seconds and traveling a distance of 852 ft.

8. With a vision to "build a car for the great multitude," Henry Ford launched his Ford Motor Company in 1903. Five years after rolling out the first Model T in 1908, using new production techniques, electrically driven machinery, and the world's first moving assembly line, the Ford Motor Company had the capability to produce a Model T in only 93 minutes.

Using just these examples as representative of the scope of inventions and innovations that changed the world, we need to consider what among them constitutes the common denominator. Let's consider a few possibilities.

Was it simply genius?	Sometimes it is a matter simply of paying attention. Lippershey's telescope, for example, resulted from two children who told him that they could see farther after playing with two lenses at his optical shop.
Is it that they made things cheaper for their customers?	Not necessarily. Newcomen's steam engine was exorbitantly expensive for its time, yet a wide range of customers recognized its value and put it to use.
Was it a matter of their superb individual expertise?	That conclusion would have to dismiss the many contributions of Edison's assistants. This conclusion would also have to question why Bell had to fight off numerous challenges to his telephone patents.
Was it simply a matter of continuing to work within an inventor's particular industry?	Designing the concept of interchangeable parts in the manufacture of rifles is clearly not a continuation of Whitney's contribution to the farming industry.
How about simply continuing advances within a particular industry?	Although Gutenberg introduced many innovative features in his printing press, the central concept—a screw press—was a stock component of wine making dating back to the Romans.
How about simply applying technology from one industry to another?	Re-application of technology is not always successful. Samuel Langley, for instance, would have flown a decade before the Wright Brothers, had his $50,000 aerodrome not crashed owing to the steam engine he had mounted on it for propulsion.
Was it a matter of ready transition and acceptance within the affected industry?	Disruptions are not necessarily welcomed within the affected industry. For instance, Ford was deemed a traitor by fellow industrialists for giving workers higher wages as an inducement to buy his cars.

What we are left to conclude is a sole common denominator: The innovator observed the opportunity to redefine the core elements of an industry—how the work was done, what was being produced, and who the market was or could be. Whether living in the days leading up to the Renaissance in Europe, the midst of the Industrial Revolution in Britain or America, the early days of the twentieth century, or the first decades of the twenty-first, these examples validate a simple truth: Opportunity for innovation and the consequent disruption of industries abound.

This truism is equally, if not more, true today. As the oft-quoted statement from Bill Gates succinctly puts it, "Never before in history has innovation offered promise of so much to so many in so short a time." It has only been a matter of decades that have seen the evolution from room-sized punch-card units powered by vacuum tubes to hand-held computing devices; yet, that dynamic shift, in turn, engendered more change and disruption. For example, only 30 years after Motorola produced the first hand-held mobile phone, Motorola's market and industry leadership were essentially dismantled with introduction of the iPhone.

As a recent study of the American market announced, in 1964 a company on the S&P 500 could, on average, expect to remain in that rarified company for 33 years. However, by 2016, the average tenure on the S&P 500 had dropped to 24 years and was "forecast to shrink to just 12 years by 2017." That report went on to project that challenged by changing markets triggered by disruptions "at the current churn rate, about half of S&P 500 companies will be replaced over the next ten years" (Anthony et al. 2018).

The challenge is being prepared to take advantage of the opportunities, to understand what needs to be done and how to transform your company. Often, such opportunities are lost, not as a consequence of a lack of recognition, but owing to a short-sighted strategy that focuses on limited, process-by-process enhancement techniques such as LEAN and Six Sigma rather than pursuing a comprehensive transformation. Placing process enhancement in historical context will highlight why employing our transformation methodology rather than remaining in the grasp of a process-by-process improvement strategy is the better path in this era of ongoing and accelerated industrial disruptions.

Predicate 2: Industry Must Step beyond Process-by-Process Improvement

To place the contemporary enthusiasm for mistaking process-by-process improvement methodologies for transformation in context, we need, briefly, to start back at the Industrial Revolution.

The Industrial Revolution changed Britain and the United States from agrarian societies with service industries largely consisting of small—often family run—businesses into a society in which production was centralized within massive factories, unskilled workers were replaced by specialized labor, and production was mechanized and powered by machines rather than by people.

Major industries, such as textile, steel production, and the railroads, were transformed. Textile production was advanced first by the flying shuttle, a weaving machine that doubled the previous average productivity of a worker, and then by the "spinning jenny," which increased productivity eight-fold. At essentially the same time, Richard Arkwright, a barber and wigmaker, figured out how to hook up a spinning machine to a water wheel. His factory, opened along the River Derwent, aided by actions by Parliament outlawing the import of cotton cloth from India, further revolutionized production by introducing a machine that took raw cotton in at one end and produced cloth out the other.

A similar pattern of successive enhancements was evidenced in the iron industry. Iron was used in much of the equipment and tools produced in Great Britain. By the eighteenth century, ironmongers were pursuing means to make iron stronger and less expensive. In relatively short succession, the discovery of adding carbon to iron produced steel, which over time became cheaper, more available, and reduced Britain's reliance on Europe.

Likewise, advancing Newcomen's design, James Watt developed a steam engine that added a rotary motion to the reciprocal up-and-down motion, a change that redefined the railroad industry. Previously using vehicles drawn by horses, the railroads transitioned to using steam engines when George Stephenson, a self-taught engineer who learned his trade by repairing textile mill steam engines, used a steam-driven locomotive on a railway line he built between Liverpool and Manchester.

Convergence of these developments—growth of the textile industry, consolidating work activities within large factories, development of the steam engine, and introduction of steam-powered machines— complemented by increasing need for specialized labor—represented the culmination of over a century of industrial innovation and disruption in Britain. At the same time, the growth of industry attracted large numbers of people to the new industrial cities, increased trade across the globe, and all but eradicated the competing small family businesses.

Although starting somewhat later than in Britain, the Industrial Revolution in America followed a very similar path to that which occurred in Britain. The farming and textile industries were revolutionized by Eli Whitney's cotton gin and Cyrus McCormick's harvester. At the same time, Watt's rotary steam engine—complemented by such innovations as the airbrake—was put to work in American railroads and in paddle wheels along the Mississippi River.

Numerous industries, aided by high protective tariffs as had occurred in Britain, were redefining the American industrial landscape as well as the American workforce. As was evidenced in England, displaced workers began a mass migration to the cities where factories were multiplying. This displaced population was augmented by thousands of immigrants from Western and Eastern Europe who saw America as the land of opportunity. The challenge now became how to take the fullest advantage, the greatest potential for profit, not only from increasingly automated industries but also from making workers more efficient.

As industries grew and factory work expanded throughout the remaining decades of the nineteenth century and early into the twentieth, the business world's focus on improved productivity began to broaden into a concentration not only on continued introduction of new inventions and equipment but also on increasing human productivity. Armed with degrees in mechanical engineering and personal observation gained from his work experience as foreman, master mechanic, chief draftsman, chief engineer, general superintendent, general manager, auditor, and head of a sales department, Frederick Winslow Taylor sought to address this question of how to improve human efficiency.

His conclusions were that a series of overarching challenges were facing American industry: a less than suitably motivated or capable workforce; a management ill-prepared to motivate greater productivity; an ineffective corporate organizational structure; and a serious disconnect between worker productivity and wages. After 26 years of refining these perceptions and experimenting with solutions while consulting for a broad array of firms—most notably Bethlehem Steel—he reported his conclusions in two seminal works that for half a century thereafter dominated the practice and philosophy of industrial engineering: *Shop Management* (1903) and *The Principles of Scientific Management* (1911).

Stated simply, as Dr. Taylor asserted, management's role was rigidly to enforce efficiency of work: instituting the "science" of scientific management; displacing previous "rule of thumb" approximations; selecting and training workers; monitoring performance; and maintaining shop discipline. As opposed to "ordinary" management where workers had control, Taylor expected "a full-half" of the work ostensibly to be owned by management accomplished through the agency of a centralized planning organization.

Professing support for the average worker and asserting that the best interests of workers and management were the same, Taylor laid out his theory of "task management," or scientific management, to which it is more commonly referred. Taylor's goal, as described in the introduction to *Shop Management* by Henry Towne (a colleague and author of a related work, *The Engineer as an Economist*) was simple:

"The substitution of machinery for unaided human labor was the great industrial achievement of the nineteenth century. The new achievement to which Dr. Taylor points the way consists in elevating human labor itself to a higher plane of efficiency and of earning power". (Taylor 1947)

The means by which this "elevation" was to be achieved involved, as Taylor explained, three major components:

1. Substituting science for the individual judgment of the workman
2. Scientifically selecting and developing workers
3. Cooperation between management and workers

As the name would imply, "task management" was predicated on providing workers with very explicit and precise instructions for every aspect of their job. These task descriptions were developed by "time-study men," who, equipped "merely with a stop-watch and a properly ruled notebook," observed a number of men completing a particular task and then, by eliminating "all false movements, slow movements, and useless movements," established work standards that all workers were thereafter expected to meet.

As significant as was the impact of scientific management, Taylor recognized that his work represented the early cusp of a societal upheaval. His expectation for the future was clear:

> The writer feels that management is to become more of an art.... Management will be studied as an art and will rest upon well recognized, clearly defined, and fixed principles instead of depending on more or less hazy ideas received from a limited observation of the few organizations with which the individual may have come in contact. (Taylor 1947)

The quest for enhanced productivity and efficiency continued to expand over the decades following issuance of Taylor's two books, spreading well beyond the confines of factory walls in large measure as a consequence of the "Commission on Economy and Efficiency in Government Service" empaneled by President Taft. The several hundred page report of the Commission released in 1912 had far-reaching implications that are still evident today.

Two million dollars a year was projected to be saved through standardizing administrative processes, installing "labor-saving" devices in government offices, eliminating or consolidating numerous federal bureaus and agencies, and centralizing federal procurement. Additionally, the Commission proposed several enduring changes to the business of government, including codifying the requirement for an annual federal budget; increasing the number of senior government positions requiring Senate confirmation; and consolidating audit functions within the Department of the Treasury.

Over the next few decades, the concept of scientific management held sway over most work in industrial engineering. Enhanced and new tools such as Gantt Charts that translated the sequence of activities comprising a project into a single depiction were produced that reinforced the principles of scientific management.

Time and motion studies also were enhanced. After meeting with Taylor, Frank Gilbreth and his wife, Lillian, began conducting motion studies using stop-motion cameras to capture, delineate, and catalog the smallest of eye, hand, and foot motions (referred to by them as "therbligs"). Most famously these detailed analyses were used to redefine processes that increased the rate of laying bricks from 1,000 a day to 2,700 by introducing a scaffold that delivered bricks at waist level rather than requiring bricklayers continually bending over to pick up bricks off the ground and by documenting the benefits of using nurses to hand surgeons instruments rather than having surgeons momentarily disrupt an operation in order to find and retrieve surgical instruments (Ferguson n.d.).

Yet, what is equally important about the work of the Gilbreths was their role in advancing the evolution of scientific management. Whereas Taylor had all but dismissed the concept of worker involvement in the planning or design of work, the Gilbreths were using their motion studies to make work easier, less taxing on the worker, as well as more productive. Infusing Taylor's concepts with an interest in what we now call ergonomics, Lillian—who later in life was to become the first tenured, woman professor in the engineering department at Purdue—introduced the formal study of the psychology of management. This interest in psychology and behavior as a contributing factor in efficiency and performance was intensified and made more prominent in industry and within the discipline of industrial engineering in the following decades by the Hawthorne experiments.

Conducted between 1924 and 1932 at Western Electric Company's Hawthorne Works in Chicago, the experiments—often described as the most important social science experiments ever conducted in an industrial setting—were initially designed to determine whether changes in lighting at the factory would contribute to greater productivity. With an eye to encouraging industries to convert to artificial lighting, the tests were expected to demonstrate that as lighting was increased, production would increase as well—and, conversely, when dimmed, productivity would decrease. When productivity increased in both instances, researchers went looking for other influencing variables.

Over a number of years and using a variety of testing scenarios, all tested conditions—changes in work schedules, pay, work environment, and worker interaction—resulted in increased productivity and expressions of increased worker satisfaction. The conclusion ultimately reached was that what contributed most directly to worker satisfaction—and thereby to worker productivity—was the workers' sense that management was interested in and paying attention to them.

As significant as were the experiments at the Western Electric manufacturing plant, this one factory has another reason it is consequential in the history and development of industrial science and industrial psychology. The three men who were to become the most prominent voices in quality and performance management all worked at the Hawthorne facility. In the years between World Wars I and II, Joseph M. Juran, W. Edward Deming, and Walter A. Shewhart were all employees of Western Electric.

Crippled by World War II, Japan sought out the assistance of both Juran and Deming to help rebuild its economy. The forces at work in turning around the Japanese economy in the years roughly from 1952 to 1980 went largely unnoticed outside of Japan for several decades. However, as the U.S. economic growth began to sputter in the 1970s and Japan became an industrial powerhouse rivaling America's stature as a world leader in many areas of production such as steel, the need to reinvigorate the American economy became increasingly urgent.

The resulting emergence of quality control and statistical process control as foundational attributes of American industry can be traced to a particular date: January 24, 1980. That was the date that NBC aired a "white paper" entitled "If Japan Can, Why Can't We?" The majority of the broadcast was an indictment of contemporary American industry:

- Industry operating with outdated and aged equipment
- Overbearing and stifling government involvement and regulation
- A management attitude mired in outmoded thinking
- Tension rather than cooperation between government and industry
- Poor management/worker relations
- A tendency to discourage creativity and innovation
- A risk adverse approach to strategic thinking
- Limited employee training and engagement in planning.

The broadcast ended on a sobering note: Unless America solved its problem of an impoverished productivity rate and poor product quality, "our children will be the first [American] generation to live worse than their parents." The only practical means of rescuing the American economy, as asserted by the broadcast, was to institute in American industries the same processes Deming had brought to Japan ("If Japan Can, Why Can't We?" n.d.).

Just as Taylor's scientific management had captured the business imagination in the early part of the twentieth century, so a single NBC documentary set in motion a wholesale, national initiative on quality and efficiency that enveloped America in the closing decades of the twentieth century and beyond. From thereon, the primary options for reinvigorating corporations were accomplished via LEAN management, Six Sigma data analysis, or—alternatively—by committing to strategic transformations.

Predicate 3: Transformations Require a Timely and Readily Implementable Methodology

Irrespective of whether your corporation chooses to engage in a limited operational overhaul or a comprehensive transformation, a straightforward and readily accomplishable process must be employed. The question, then, is what process does the company use? Our process proceeds in a disciplined manner: deciding whether a transformation is warranted; examining the mechanics of the process; detailing the roles and responsibilities of all the communities involved—company leadership, the workforce, the board of directors, and independent review teams; and then completing project commissioning, the final step leading to opening the doors to your transformed company. To provide additional context, chapter discussions include examples of specific challenges encountered by actual U.S., Canadian, and British projects accompanied by introduction of tools and forms we have successfully employed in transformations we have led.

Our experience dates back to 1988 when we competed in the first year of the Malcolm Baldrige National Quality Award competition; the award was established as part of the Malcolm Baldrige National Quality Improvement Act, passed by President Ronald Reagan. The goal, as stated in the "Findings and Purposes Section" of Public Law 100-107, was to highlight the reality that process improvement, strategic planning, quality control, and worker engagement were essential in sustaining the country's economic base.

Since that time we have been engaged in and led various activities associated with promoting quality and efficiency. We have participated in and overseen LEAN events; as Six Sigma Champions, we have designed and monitored Six Sigma analyses and the assessment of Black Belt candidates. Projects we have supported in strategic planning and transformation include major corporations in both the United States and the UK; state school boards; government and not-for-profit agencies; and multi-billion-dollar federally funded projects. All of this experience and expertise was coalesced into the process described in this text during a transformation review we recently conducted that entailed a corporation's entire spectrum of functions—administrative, business, engineering, safety, and operations—a review that produced more than 50 transformational initiatives contributing to the successful redefinition of the company.

The first two chapters of the book examine the business context—understanding the differences between the business implications of operational improvements and transformation along with our approach for anticipating and appreciating the transformation's demands—in particular what it will mean to the company and to the company's customer base. Following those discussions, Chapters 3, 4, and 5 detail the roles, responsibilities, and the processes to be employed by the company leadership, the workers, and the company's board of directors, respectively. The final chapter, Chapter 6, describes the concluding steps in completing the transformation—the transitioning into the newly redefined corporation.

It is this comprehensive methodology and the dozens of tools and practices detailed in this text that will in total provide you with *The Practical Guide to Transforming Your Company*.

CHAPTER 1

Transformation—Getting Started

There is only one valid definition of business purpose: to create a customer.... Because it is its purpose to create a customer, any business enterprise has two—and only these two—basic functions: marketing and innovation. They are the entrepreneurial functions.

—Peter Drucker
The Practice of Management, 1954

Many types of changes can be implemented in a company in order to sustain and promote its economic stability. At one level there are the changes made to individual programs and processes. Broadening that approach to address essentially all the company programs—through such measures as enhanced performance monitoring, statistical analysis, and/or the development of tracking methods utilized in the observation of work—can bring about a redefinition of the operational basis for the company. In contrast, overhauling the very core of the company, committing to an enterprise-wide transformation, is a much larger and more involved voyage—challenging the company's existing long-term strategy and essentially all the associated processes, programs, and protocols.

As a first step in deciding whether that level of commitment, a readiness to tackle the foundational elements of the company, is appropriate, a clear understanding is needed of the consequences and implications of undertaking a transformation. Being that all three redesign options—pursuing localized improvements in performance, operational redefinition, and transformations—arise from a common heritage, an abbreviated history of performance management is the best means to clarify the principal differences among these three courses for making substantive revisions to the company.

Placing Transformations in Historical Context

In the years between World Wars I and II, Joseph M. Juran, W. Edward Deming, and Walter A. Shewhart, all employees of Western Electric, became prominent voices in the development and implementation of quality and performance management. Shewhart ushered in the era of statistical process analysis with the introduction of the development of process control charts that detailed percentages of defective parts, supported projections of future system performance, and helped identify causes of and remedies for the defects. Juran, who worked as a chief industrial engineer, introduced a variety of quality tools (such as the Pareto Principle—also known as the 80/20 rule), but was most influential in institutionalizing the quality movement. In what is commonly referred to as the "Juran Trilogy," he advocated: (1) quality planning, understanding customer needs and defining processes, products, and services to respond to those needs; (2) quality control, monitoring production with specific focus on identifying and correcting causes of defects; and (3) quality improvement, a continued pursuit of making products better and more responsive to customer needs.

Deming, in turn, synthesized the use of statistical process control, quality improvement, and engaging workers as agents in improving system performance into a single ethic. Encapsulated in his 14 points of management, Deming highlighted the need for re-examining work from a fresh perspective; continuous quality improvement; promoting customer loyalty and worker motivation; cultivating worker/ management cooperation and collaboration; taking action on confirmed knowledge to improve processes; and aggressively reducing all forms of waste.

The Shewhart, Juran, and Deming lineage was born out of declining industrial markets, competitive economies, and the lack of advancements in disruptive innovation. With rising political and global economic pressures, as was made evident in a number of public laws passed by Congress in the latter part of the twentieth century, it was clear that:

1. American business and industry were beginning to understand that poor quality cost companies as much as 20 percent of sales revenues

nationally and that improved quality of goods and services goes hand in hand with improved productivity, lower costs, and increased profitability.

2. Strategic planning for quality and quality improvement programs, through commitment to excellence in manufacturing and services, was becoming more and more essential to corporate well-being in a dynamic economy and to the ability to compete effectively in the global marketplace.

3. Improved management understanding of worker participation and involvement in quality was essential as well as the recognition that greater emphasis on statistical process control contributed directly to dramatic improvements in the cost and quality of products and services.

As the advancement of tracking metrics and total quality management were introduced into best practices among businesses, industry, and government, two predominant and enduring schools of thought regarding the preferred methodology for assessing quality efficiency and system performance evolved: (1) Six Sigma, principally aligned with Deming's emphasis on statistical process control, and (2) the LEAN process, principally reflecting Juran's quality trilogy. Each of the methodologies in its own way was designed to wage war on what were generally agreed to by the two competing schools as seven potential sources of waste in any process (Table 1.1).

Table 1.1 Seven sources of waste in industry

1.	Defects	Wasted effort involved in inspecting for and fixing defects
2.	Overproduction	Waste resulting from production exceeding demand
3.	Transport	Excess movement of parts, supplies, or products not required to perform the processing
4.	Waiting	Waste associated with waiting for the next production step: interruptions or disruptions in production
5.	Inventory	Inventory accumulated in excess of what is needed to complete production of orders
6.	Motion	People, equipment, or supplies moving more times than are required to perform the processing
7.	Processing	Unnecessary processing activity owing to poor tool or product design

The LEAN process, often referred to as the Toyota Way, focuses on improving the general flow of a process by eliminating these defects and sources of waste. An outgrowth of Juran's approach of involving the workforce in the improvement process, LEAN embodies the concepts of quality circles (small teams or work groups formed to analyze and improve work practices) and the related concept of total quality management, a movement promoted by Armand Feigenbaum in the 1950s, which encouraged engaging entire organizations in quality initiatives and then charging workers with responsibility for continuous improvement within their respective workplaces.

Relying on this democratized approach to quality improvement and enhanced efficiency, LEAN can be said to be consisting of five essential principles accomplished through a select set of readily applied tools:

1. Challenge: establishing and assessing progress in achieving the vision and goals established for the organization
2. Continuous improvement: acknowledging that every process can be improved and that settling for the status quo or accepting a standard of "good enough" is not acceptable
3. Informed decision making: making decisions based on first-hand knowledge, which can only be gained by engaging with workers in their work environment
4. Respect: taking every stakeholder's and worker's problems seriously and engaging personnel as equal partners in promoting and achieving continuous improvement
5. Teamwork: developing individuals through collaborative engagement in problem-solving and by recognizing individuals' contributions and capabilities

To put these principles into practice, LEAN relies primarily on a facilitator who assists a team in identifying and evaluating improvement opportunities using a limited number of easy-to-apply tools. Foremost of the tools and the heart of LEAN is having the team produce a process map. Each step in the process is recorded on a sticky note and then these notes are arranged on wall-mounted charts—first arranged to reflect the process as currently performed, and then, by adding, removing, or repositioning the steps to produce the proposed, improved process. By placing steps above or below a ruled line, the process map is also used to gain team consensus on which steps add value and which ones do not.

Once the new process sequence is determined, the LEAN team conducts a brief period of monitoring and data collection to confirm the effectiveness and improved performance (often calculated as cost savings) resulting from replacing the existing system with the new model. The final outcome of the effort is a redesigned process, ready for implementation, and—most valued by LEAN—a process that has been developed by and is "owned" by the people who run the process rather than a process that had been dictated to them by management.

In contrast, Six Sigma, advancing and predicated on the work of Deming, is a data-driven approach that seeks to drive out any process defects (essentially any condition outside the customer's expectations) ultimately striving to reduce the number of defects to no more than 3.4 per million opportunities (an opportunity being any aspect of the process susceptible to performance weaknesses). Although the Six Sigma methodology is often described in simple terms as DMAIC or DMADV (define, measure, analyze, improve, control; or define, measure, analyze, design, verify), implementation is anything but simple, easy, or given to immediate results.

Having gained its momentum primarily from implementation at Motorola and General Electric (GE), Six Sigma analyses are rigorously executed by a hierarchy of extensively trained personnel. Simple assignments may be done by personnel referred to as "Green Belts"; more sophisticated analyses, often lasting months, are conducted by "Black Belts" under the tutelage of "Master Black Belts" (personnel who have received formal Black Belt certification). In addition to these practitioners, progress in all Six Sigma projects is monitored by "Six Sigma Champions," generally senior company managers who have received abbreviated training.

In contrast to the limited training given to the Six Sigma Champions, training for Green Belts may require weeks; Black Belt training is on the order of 4 months. Or, alternatively, using the model introduced at GE in 1998 to engage the entire workforce in using the process, and not unlike Deming's approach of giving all employees instruction in basic statistical methods, Jack Welch, the company's chairman at the time, required all exempt employees to complete a 13-day, 100-hour Six Sigma training program.

The reason for such extensive training is that unlike the approaches in LEAN that rely on tools requiring minimal training to apply, Six Sigma utilizes sophisticated analytical tools. Beyond such basic tools as process mapping and control charts, Six Sigma's tools require extensive training and computational resources to apply and interpret correctly. (For example, one commonly employed tool is an Analysis of Variance used to test hypotheses to determine whether or not an event or defect is a function of random variation.) Stated as a simple comparison, Six Sigma is predicated on an engineered solution to eliminating waste; LEAN, on the other hand, is predicated on the use of a teamed approach to developing a consensual agreement on implementable process enhancements.

However effective these two methodologies are in producing more efficient processes, they may not serve a company well if, indeed, the need is for a more dramatic change to the business's core in order to ensure sustained profitability. Localized process enhancement, whether the result of Six Sigma or LEAN, has a limited impact on the company as a whole:

1. Localized process enhancement often emphasizes and secures enhanced efficiency or quality improvement for the sake of quality improvement instead of tying improvements to the corporate bottom line.
2. Localized process enhancement tends to focus on improvements within departments or business functions, not among them.
3. Localized process enhancement is most often performed independent of and unaligned with any articulated vision of the overall goals or ambitions of the company.

In today's extremely competitive economic environment, survival and corporate prosperity may demand more than localized process enhancement: it demands not merely a process-by-process set of enhancements but, rather, a more global overhaul, that is, an enterprise-wide transformation.

To prepare against market turbulence, Huron—a firm devoted to assisting corporations in anticipating and responding to industry disruptions—suggests five activities, the last three of which diverge from the underlying assumptions of scientific management, Six Sigma, and LEAN:

1. Pay attention to new trends, products, and services
2. Focus on changing customer behaviors
3. Assume that tomorrow may not resemble today
4. Assess the cost of inaction
5. Embrace transformation (Anthony et al. 2018)

Further, as explained in a 2012 article in the *Harvard Business Review*, changes in companies, as we noted, take three distinct forms: operational enhancement, transformation of the company's operational model, and strategic transformation (Gilbert, Evring, and Foster 2012).

Operational enhancement, which is a clear descendent of all the efficiency and quality initiatives just discussed, involves doing what the company has already been doing but doing it better, solving performance problems, and reducing inefficiencies. The goal is to lower costs, increase profits, and increase customer satisfaction.

Transformation of the operational model introduces a fundamental change in the core business: While remaining in the same industry, the company reinvents itself. Strategic transformation, in contrast, represents a total rethinking of what the company is, what it does, who its customer base is, and where it is going. For example, in an operational enhancement, a newspaper firm might automate production tasks previously performed manually. Relying on those types of changes and some realignment of markets, an operational transformation of the newspaper might entail broadening its services to add online multimedia capabilities.

As compared to the operational enhancement and the operational transformation, a strategic transformation redefines the foundations of the corporation. In such a case, the newspaper might consider transforming itself into a producer of fine art imprints—a rebranding achieved through retooling the production lines, introducing new technology, retraining the workforce, and acquiring companies already well positioned in the art reproduction market.

These differing forms of enhancement and transformation are not, as evident, of equal impact on the company and its workforce or equal in challenge as regards the demands of implementation. Operational efforts focus on creating parity with competitors. The operational model involves committing to a redefinition as regards what constitutes successful corporate performance. Strategic transformation, in comparison, requires wholesale reorientation of the core business.

Depending on the current circumstance of the company and industry, complemented by knowledge gained using the five steps Huron advocates for assessing and surviving potential industry disruptions, a company can choose among the three forms of change or can combine efforts to achieve a step function adjustment in operation followed by a more global transformation.

Preliminary Planning

As a first step in starting to think through a transformation, a core review process, assigned to an integrated team of management and workers, should be used to fully understand the implications. This understanding begins with reassessing a number of factors: what is the source of requirements that define the work processes and products; whether those requirements are externally imposed (i.e., regulations) or they represent engineered and administrative controls developed by management and the technical staff; where do opportunities exist for improving performance; where are the most common and most consequential process problems; and what is the perceived sense of customer satisfaction with the company's products and services.

This core review not only is important from the standpoint of gaining perspective that will be invaluable in determining a path forward; it also is the initial message to all employees that it is acceptable to challenge the status quo, and, importantly, that challenge is not synonymous with being negative. If this common objective is effectively communicated, the process will naturally enhance the level of transparency and cooperation among the various levels of worker and management. Performing reviews from the perspective of improving production and sustainability, looking candidly at the potential alternative pathways for the company going forward, and proceeding in a disciplined manner will also be important in aiding in reducing the emotional attachment that people have to the systems with which they have become comfortable.

Whether the company plans an operational transformation or an enterprise-wide strategic transformation, the core review must be complemented by firm and unwavering commitments by management and a straightforward, readily accomplishable process.

Understanding the Corporate Predicates

Often senior leadership teams have a basic understanding of what the company vision is, but do not have a fundamental perspective of how to translate that message to the first-line supervisory level and/or the workforce. This common disconnect is why it is critical to ensure that the company vision is clearly defined and that a formal process is introduced to transform the vision into a cohesive approach to implementation. Practical exercises geared to help assess existing processes, trigger discussions regarding areas that can be reworked to be more effective, and define team actions that will translate into tangible, recognized enhancement are the essence of the core review.

The key is to know and understand what your company does, how it does it, and where the opportunities lie. Although this knowledge should be immediately apparent, often, over time, the bases on which the company was built or the practices upon which it relies remain stable while the business environment is changing—potentially invalidating the company's assumptions about products, services, customers, and the market.

What is required is a fundamental understanding of how the company/organization operates. Is it flexible, efficient, and responsive to change? What we have found is that one of the underlying reasons companies become disconnected from their origins over time is there is a subculture within the company that adjusts to and/or works around ineffectual systems and processes, a subculture that learns it is acceptable to skirt requirements that no longer apply or that are perceived as no longer adding value. The resulting consequence of the growth of such a subculture is not improved or sustained efficiency, but, rather, an expanding band of inefficiency; it is an inefficiency characterized by such features as continued issuance of unnecessary reports, work-arounds that increase waste, jeopardized quality and safety, and increased labor costs. Having become the accepted norms, these processes are often accompanied by layers of inflated controls and procedures instituted in response to production problems, process delays, and audit findings.

Continuing on this path—avoiding what is needed or bolting on new initiatives and controls—eventually creates a working environment in which employees improvise processes, eliminating standardization and quality controls while also further eroding interorganizational communication and coordination.

Yet, what must be recognized is that underlying these issues remains a workforce that typically remains committed to the company's success; the introduction of work-arounds and departures from the original practices and processes is intended to support, not weaken, the company or its market performance. Despite the good intentions, once a process and/or requirement has been codified, the assertion that "we have always done it this way" is often sufficient to sustain the practice whether or not it is the best means of accomplishing the task or in the best interests of the company.

Righting the Course

Transformation—whether putting the company back on solid ground or pursuing an enterprise-wide redefinition—begins with re-integrating the work practices, establishing a work environment that encourages process improvement, establishing a clear-cut vision of where the company is going, providing explicit expectations, and engaging the workforce in delivering on the vision.

During core reviews conducted as part of our businesses' planning for a transformation, we have been routinely made aware that upper management relies heavily on analysis and status reports but is not as intensely attuned to the fact that the workforce already knows of areas where work can be done more strategically, where cost and schedule enhancements can be made, and where opportunities to increase the likelihood of the transformation's success exist. One of the keys to a successful transformation is recognizing that the process must take full advantage of the company's resources, cumulative experience, and expertise.

Transforming and/or redefining the company demands tools and techniques predicated on performance enhancement methodologies such as LEAN, Six Sigma, and total quality management. Yet, prior to performing a core business review, the management team must recognize the benefits of purposeful change and be willing to create and support a vision for that change.

Establishing a tangible vision of what constitutes success for any transformed core business organization must come with a clear set of expectations and a realistic appreciation of the challenges in delivering on those expectations.

Challenges in the form of questioning and requiring specifics of the leadership's expectations will come from within the organization, often from first-line supervisors or management. Such challenges do not arise because these levels of management do not want to support new initiatives; rather, the need for precision and detail at this level of the company occurs because this is where "the rubber meets the road." Only with a sufficient level of detail provided by the company leadership can this community be effective in its job: ascertaining precisely the breadth and depth of work demanded by the transformation; communicating with and gaining support of the workforce; engaging in translating management initiatives into work practices; and, ultimately, delivering on the leadership's vision.

With this observation in mind, company leadership has to be sensitive in recognizing the process by which the transformation is actually delivered. Early on when the concept of the transformation is being developed, senior management should engage an influential and broadly respected individual from each major organization to participate in the transformation process; while assisting in delivering the leadership's messages, this individual will also serve as a voice of the workers who will be implementing the transformation. Yet, relying exclusively on these individuals to spread and inculcate the messages is not sufficient; in coordination with these representatives of the workforce, leadership should hold town halls, have brown-bag lunch discussions, and schedule open forums to discuss the new vision and how the transformation will be conducted.

In thinking through the conceptual stages of the transformation, the company leadership should ensure that proposed changes are purposeful and sustainable. Otherwise the "old way" of doing things will creep back into the organization due to lack of sustained support. It is also important that leadership does not unintentionally begin adding requirements or restraints that will redirect the energy from the primary expectations of the transformation. As we will be discussing in later chapters, the transformation process—like LEAN and other enhancement methodologies—must be understood in large measure by the workers implementing the new vision.

Furthering the idea of not distracting from the challenging work of the transformation, using recommendations from the core review, the leadership should evaluate whether existing requirements can be temporarily or permanently suspended. Any actions that can strongly communicate an intention to minimize distractions, avoid wasted energy, or that can promote an "all in" commitment to the transformation should be considered. In other words, messages must be accompanied by actions: Send a clear message that the leadership understands the challenges, is committed to the transformation, and sees the path forward as a collaborative endeavor.

Getting the Transformation Underway

It is evident, even in advance of exploring the specific attributes of the process as will be addressed in subsequent chapters, that operational redefinition and/or transformation do not necessarily require an immediate overhaul of all program elements. Yet, even if a phased approach is to be implemented, there must be a "buy-in" of the support and implementation of change, large and small, from upper level management to the warehouse person, in order to be successful.

As a consequence of the core review, it may be determined that the organizational skill mix does not align with the specific demands and disciplines required by the new transformation. This does not necessarily mean that mass layoffs are required. However, what it might indicate is that there needs to be organizational adjustments and personnel development programs in order to deliver the transformed company. These needs include such considerations as investment in cross-training among programs and disciplines; merging organizational units to reflect changed requirements or redesigned processes and protocols; and re-evaluating the management structure to promote changes in work cultures and work environments. The important factor is to recognize, with sufficient time to respond, that a transformation is more than the redesign of isolated processes, but a major shift in the character of the company.

As daunting as some of this may sound, there are several activities that can be done in parallel with the core review that can help get the transformation started. Creating a communication plan should be done in parallel with creating the new vision. During the initial formulation of the vision, it is also important to construct the basic organization that will lead the transformation. As with any project, individuals need to be identified who have the authority and accountability for moving the project forward. Supporting these people should be a team consisting of individuals who are known to have influence at the various levels of the company. These team members, also selected in the early stages of formulating the visions, may or may not come from managerial positions, but, rather, should be selected based on knowledge, experience, influence with co-workers, and communication skills.

Having given consideration to what to expect from a transformation in general, the next logical step is to begin looking at what your particular transformation will entail. As we have suggested in this chapter, central to the transformation is the vision and the associated expectations for the company and its staff.

To that end, Chapter 2 will explain the process for effectively previewing the transformation, getting a glimpse of such factors as impacts on the customer base. Then, having clear definition of the vision and the expectations, we will proceed with exploring the roles, responsibilities, and practices expected from each of the three major communities: the company leadership, the workforce, and the board of directors.

CHAPTER 2

Previewing the Transformation—Paving the Road to Success

"Would you tell me, please, which way I ought to go from here?"
"That depends a good deal on where you want to get to," said the Cat.
"I don't care where—" said Alice.
"Then it doesn't much matter which way you go," said the Cat.
"—so long as I get somewhere," Alice added as an explanation.
"Oh, you're sure to do that," said the Cat, "if you only walk long enough."
—Lewis Carroll, *Alice's Adventures in Wonderland*, 1869

Putting the Project in Perspective

In 2002, the United Kingdom (UK) undertook an initiative to overhaul the record-keeping component of the National Health Service (NHS). With the laudatory goals of transitioning to a nationally integrated system of electronic records, the initiative known as the NHS National Programme for IT (NPfIT) (subsequently rebranded as "Connecting for Health") sought to deliver a nation-wide capability that would provide: (a) an integrated electronic health records system; (b) electronic prescriptions; (c) an electronic appointment booking system; and (d) an IT infrastructure with sufficient capacity to support and link both national applications and local health systems.

The origins of the concept derived from a 90-minute meeting at Downing Street chaired by then prime minister, Tony Blair. Enamored with the concept of delivering a massive win for the Liberals in advance of the 2005 election, the prime minister initiated what was to be a 3-year,

£6.4 billion project. In contrast, the project was ultimately scrapped some 10 years after the Downing Street meeting, having delivered only limited components of the project and having incurred essentially a 100-percent overrun of the originally anticipated budget—a final cost of approximately £12 billion. It was, in the words of a 2013 report issued by the Public Accounts Committee (PAC)—a select committee of the British House of Commons responsible for overseeing government expenditures to ensure they are effective and honest—one of the "worst and most expensive contracting fiascos" in public sector history.

The issues underlying the demise of the project were not foreign to efforts previously undertaken to improve NHS performance, nor did they go unremarked in the recommendations of government reviews conducted at the outset of implementing the Connecting for Health initiative. Notable among the failures in the immediately preceding years were (1) a regional attempt to link one district's hospital information systems, personnel management systems, and community care data—an effort that failed largely owing to ineffective management; (2) a larger-scale attempt electronically to link the records of seven regional hospitals, unsuccessful due to lack of ability to integrate data maintained in a number of incompatible computer systems; and (3) the 1992 proposed comprehensive overhaul of the entire national records program known as the Information Management and Technology (IM&T) strategy, which, while introducing some advances in records management, was undone by a lack of clear objectives and targets.

Despite these earlier costly disappointments and the fact that the dismantling of the IM&T strategy was in part the impetus for the Downing Street meeting, efforts went forward undeterred by the lack of further planning at the executive levels of government and unencumbered by the obvious lessons that should have been learned from the preceding attempts at records centralization. Nor were the efforts curtailed or delayed by reports issued by various government agencies that highlighted an array of signposts forewarning of impending problems: In addition to a lack of detailed planning, the reports noted that the project had not provided clear statements of the project's benefits or the plan for delivering on the vision; the program structure was overly complex; and stakeholder engagement had been minimal at best and had entirely omitted interaction with several major constituencies. Rather, the project pressed forward; its contracting strategy designed to expedite awards produced poorly defined, overlapping, and contradictory scopes of work distributed among a host of companies—a prescription for failure compounded by the unrestrained and unchecked funding driven by the governing party's arbitrary 3-year completion schedule (Champion-Awwad et al. 2014).

Consequently, the project became a case study for what we have come to understand as the 10 principal reasons why transformations fail:

- Poorly defined definition of success
- Unrealistic or poorly analyzed expectations
- Ambition outrunning capability
- Lack of clear ownership and accountability
- Lack of customer/stakeholder engagement
- Unachievable or arbitrary timelines for ill-defined deliverables
- Insufficient communication within and among project levels
- Lack of alignment between strategic vision and accomplishment of physical work
- Blindness or unwillingness to recognize when course changes are warranted
- Being unprepared for and uncommitted to the long haul (budget, resources, time, commitment)

The elements of failure evidenced by the NPfIT project are reflective of issues and breakdowns at all levels—incomplete understanding of the drivers and influences that result in pursuing enterprise transformation, the ineffective roles played by the leadership and the workers, and the arbitrary expectations regarding schedules and deliverables.

Having completed a number of transformations, we recognized the need for the entire company to develop a thorough understanding of the implications of the transformation before actually engaging in its implementation. As a consequence, over the years we have developed a straightforward means of allowing all levels of the company (leadership, board of directors, management, first-line supervision, and workers) to anticipate challenges, gain understanding of the connotations of their proposed new corporate vision, and get an appreciation of what it will take to translate the vision into reality.

In other words, we begin each company's transformation efforts with a basic self-check, an opportunity for the company to expand its understanding of, better anticipate, and preview the reality of the endeavor. The check entails three interlocked components: (1) understanding of how the company is and will be positioned within its respective industry; (2) appreciation of the decision-making methodology employed by corporate strategists; and (3) a process we call the "reasonable customer" analysis that identifies the expectations of the transformed company's external and internal customers and, thereby, provides a fundamental set of design criteria (Figure 2.1).

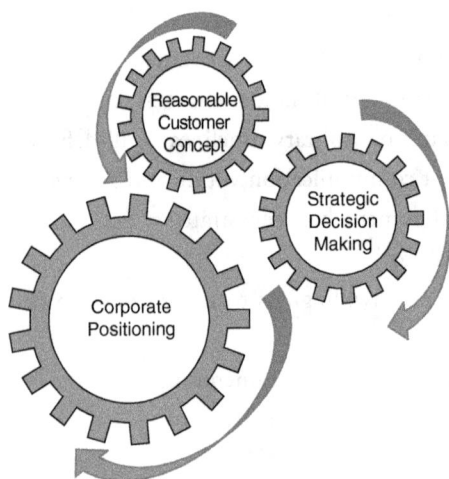

Figure 2.1 The three interlocked elements for previewing the transformation

Previewing the Transformation

Component 1: Corporate Positioning

Transformations can be triggered by a variety of circumstances, some reasonable and some political. As with the case of the UK Connect for Health initiative, the transformation was driven by a political impulse— the goal of positioning the Liberal Party for an election victory. However, as we noted, that impulse, untempered by sound planning and reasoned judgment, only succeeded in costing the UK citizens an excessive amount of money with little of value in return. A similar situation can also be the consequence of an overly ambitious corporate CEO or board of directors, whose good intentions to enhance the company's value are outpaced by the need to ensure the reasonableness and the wherewithal to accomplish the transformation.

More commonly, transformations are triggered by a leadership recognition of one of a number of situations where failure to act—failure to determine a new path for the corporation—will likely result in the significant loss of value, or, in worst cases, the demise of the company. Among the most common reasons why a transformation may be warranted are:

- Sustained loss of value (i.e., revenue, stock value, market share)
- Anticipated failure to meet projected market or financial targets/commitments
- Loss of company reputation requiring rebranding
- Protracted market instability
- Initiative undertaken to position the company to take advantage of previously unanticipated opportunities

Driven by a range of business circumstances (e.g., changes in the economy or the specific market the company is in), the company needs to rethink how to respond. At one level, as we discussed earlier, the response can focus on process enhancements, making workers more efficient through enhanced training, changing the work practices, and adjusting schedules. However, if the response effort is limited to these factors, then the plan is not in fact designed to conduct a comprehensive transformation, but, rather, company leadership is willing to retain the overall mission and vision of the company while simply improving productivity or performance.

In contrast, if the plan for responding to the challenge begins with a redefinition of the mission, a new vision for the company, then the company is committing to an enterprise-wide transformation. The flow-down in the activities to be undertaken, as depicted in Figure 2.2, translates from a goal of securing the company's long-term position, through an alignment of programs and processes, and continuing through the redefinition of worker assignments necessary to create the new or revised set of products or services (Rouse 2005).

Impetus for Transformation	Sample Initiating Factors	Hierarchy of Transformation Activities	Ownership	Ends Pursued Primary Focus of Effort	Potential Means for Achieving Transformation
– Sustained loss of value (i.e., revenue, stock value, market share) – Anticipated failure to meet projected market or financial targets / commitments – Initiative undertaken to position company to take advantage of previously unanticipated opportunities – Loss of company reputation requiring rebranding – General market are instability	Changes in the economy Enhanced / expanded competition Market decline Changes in company leadership Quality / safety problems tarnishing perception of goods / services Supply chain limitations / interruptions Outmoded technology	Redefine corporate vision /purpose / strategy / objectives	Leadership	Secure long-term corporate value and stability	Add new leadership Introduce new technology Corporate mergers / acquisitions Retool major production lines so as to produce new products Introduce new programs and processes Corporate rebranding
		↓ Program Redefinition	Manage-ment	Bring programs into alignment with new vision / strategy	
		↓ Process enhancement	Super-vision / Workers	Implement management direction / maximize quality and volume of output	
		↓ New skills / jobs / work assignments	Workers	Create the products / services envisioned in new corporate vision / strategy	

Figure 2.2 Transformation: A basic perspective

What is required to understand this first component of previewing the prospective transformation is to consider and record the company's proposed position relative to each of the columns in Figure 2.2:

1. What is causing the need for the transformation? Is that need fully understood and founded on solid information and disciplined analysis?

2. What are the principal initiating factors that need to be addressed? Are these factors within the company's control, and, if so, what are the actions that need to be taken?

3. Who, organizationally, is responsible, accountable, and authorized to implement the required actions? Is there a clear definition of what tasks and steps each action will entail? When the actions have been accomplished, how can it be demonstrated if they have been sufficient and appropriate in resolving the initiating event?

4. Is there a means to validate that the goals set for the transformed company are implementable?
5. What transactional changes, in addition to the strategic changes, are needed and how will they be accomplished?

Once these questions have been answered and recorded, the next component of the previewing process is to provide a straightforward means of adding the experience and expertise of the leadership to evaluating the appropriateness of and the ability to implement the transformation.

Component 2: Effective Strategic Decision Making

As is evident from the preceding discussion, the corporate leadership determines the new strategy. Although that is as it should be, as the NHS example makes evident, strategic, transformational plans are not always, in and of themselves, well formulated, appropriate, or achievable. Put succinctly, the path forward is dependent on (1) the leadership's inclinations—the types of solutions they innately consider appropriate; (2) their perspectives—the experiences and history they bring with them; (3) their managerial predispositions—the predicates they think most essential in gaging the efficacy of a resolution to a given technical or financial problem; and (4) their approach to decision making—the balance of intuition, creativity, and evidence they tend to employ in the process of arriving at a solution.

Although we are generally given to accept as fact that company leadership—having risen to the ranks of CEO, directors, vice presidents, and other key positions overseeing the company—is inherently capable of and prepared for setting course on a transformation, that assumption needs to be more carefully examined. As with many of the tenets of contemporary business management, this assumption and the expectations of senior leadership as adept decision makers derive from management theories promulgated in the same period as the rise of Frederick Taylor's propositions on scientific management that were discussed in the Introduction and Chapter 1.

Based largely on his personal management experience, Henri Fayol, a mining engineer who directed several major mining enterprises in France and was credited with the transformation and turnaround of a failing mining industry, developed a broadly accepted concept of administration that remains the predicate of what is assumed to be the job of management. Published in 1916, around the same time as Taylor introduced scientific management, Fayol's text *Administration Industrielle et Générale* presented a theory of management that became known internationally as Fayolism.

Fayol's text, translated into English and published in 1949 as *General and Industrial Administration*, stipulated 5 functions and 14 principles of management. As noted in the foreword of the English edition, "the demand for [the original French publication of the book] was immediate and persistent.... By 1925, 15,000 copies had been printed." Briefly reviewing these 14 principles and 5 management functions makes evident the genesis of the ongoing and sustained assumptions about what management does and how it functions. Tables 2.1 and 2.2 present summaries of Fayol's principles and management functions (Fayol 1949).

Table 2.1 Fayol's management functions

"All undertakings require planning, organization, command, co-ordination and control, and in order to function properly, all must observe the same general principles."		
1	Planning	If foresight is not the whole of management, at least it is an essential part of it. To foresee, in this context, means both to assess the future and make provision for it: the result envisaged, the line of action to be followed, the stages to go through, and methods to use.
2	Organizing	To organize a business is to provide it with everything useful to its functioning: raw materials, tools, capital, personnel. All this may be divided into two main sections, the material organization and the human organization.
3	Command	The organization, having been formed, must be set going and this is the mission of command to get the optimum return from all employees.
4	Coordination	To coordinate is to harmonize all the activities of a concern so as to facilitate its working, and its success. It is to keep expenditure proportionate to financial resources, equipment and tools to production needs, stocks to rate of consumption, sales to production.
5	Control	Control consists in verifying whether everything occurs in conformity with the plan adopted, the instructions issued, and the principles established. It has an object to point out weaknesses and errors in order to rectify them and prevent recurrence.

Table 2.2 *Fayol's principles of management*

1	Division of work	Division of work produces more and better work with the same effort. The worker, always on the same part, and the manager, concerned always with the same matters, acquire an ability, sureness, and accuracy.
2	Authority	Authority is the right to give orders and the power to exact obedience. Authority is not to be conceived of apart from responsibility; where authority is exercised, responsibility arises.
3	Discipline	Discipline is in essence obedience, application, energy, behavior, and outward marks of respect observed in accordance with the standing agreements between the firm and its employees.
4	Unity of command	Employees should receive orders from one superior only. If not, authority is undermined, discipline is in jeopardy, order disturbed, and stability threatened.
5	Unity of direction	There should be one head and one plan for a group of activities having the same objective. It is the condition essential to unity of action, coordination of strength, and focusing of effort.
6	Subordination of individual interest	In a business, the interest of one employee or group of employees should not prevail over that of the company.
7	Remuneration	Remuneration should be fair and, as far as is possible, afford satisfaction both to personnel and the company.
8	Centralization	All direction should be provided through a central administration. The objective is to pursue the optimum utilization of all faculties of the personnel.
9	Scaler chain	There must be a straight line of authority and communication extending from top management to the lowest operating ranks. The line of authority is the route all need to follow.
10	Order	There will be clear and distinct assignments for all workers and work. Work assignments should follow the logic of "the right person in the right place."
11	Equity	For the personnel to be encouraged to carry out duties with all the devotion and loyalty, personnel must be treated with kindliness and equity.
12	Stability and tenure of personnel	Time is required for an employee to get used to new work and succeed in doing it well.
13	Initiative	Thinking out a plan and ensuring its success is one of the keenest satisfactions for an intelligent man to experience. The initiative of all represents a great source of strength for businesses.
14	Esprit de corps	Harmony, union among the personnel of a concern, is great strength. Effort, then, should be made to establish it.

"Planning," the function of most immediate concern here, in the context of Fayol's work, is exclusively focused on the short-term responses to or in anticipation of need for adjustments to the current work of the company. Yet, what is not envisioned or accounted for in Fayol's construction is the concept of leadership as we understand it today—the demanding, strategic orientation and decision making that reacts to and anticipates major occurrences, opportunities, or perturbations in the market, the customer base, the sustained profitability of the corporation— circumstances that influence a re-visioning and transformation of the company. This responsibility is the differentiation between management and leadership, process enhancement and transformation.

The differentiation can also be between critical and uncritical thinking. Looking to another contemporary of Taylor and Fayol, we can gain explanation of the mechanics of how leadership makes decisions. John Dewey in his landmark work *How We Think* (1910) detailed the process inherent in how each of us, including corporate leadership, makes decisions. At the most fundamental level, the decision-making process entails five steps: (1) we recognize there is a problem, (2) we precisely define the problem, (3) we consider possible solutions, (4) we settle upon a solution, and (5) we then put the solution into effect.

As a simple example, say that it is a Friday night. You decide that you want to go out after work and do something (problem). You decide you don't want to be out too late and you don't want to drive too far (problem definition). Looking through the newspaper, you see listings of events—plays, a concert, poetry readings, and movies (possible solutions). After considering the options, you decide on a nearby movie that is a sequel to a movie you really enjoyed and is starting in 30 minutes (solution). You check the time, put on your jacket, and head to the theater (implementation).

As is evident from our personal experiences, and is true in corporate decision making, portions of this process may be done intuitively without formal study or even without conscious effort. It is that fact—the innate reliance on our experience, intuition, biases, and thought processes to arrive at reasoned conclusions—that suggests both the strength and the potential pitfalls of strategic decision making in the planning phases of a potential transformation.

Of course, corporate challenges are far more complex than our example—but complexity does not always mean that the depth of analysis (for any of the first four phases of the decision-making process) is accomplished at a level commensurate with the need fully to appreciate whether the problem is sufficiently understood, the set of potential solutions immediately applicable, or the final accepted resolution implementable. In particular, as Dewey further elucidates, a potential problem is always present because we are prone to accepting the first plausible solution that presents itself (irrespective of whether or not it is in practicality the best solution). As he explains, "essential thinking" means critical thinking:

> The easiest way is to accept any suggestion that seems plausible and thereby [eliminate] mental uneasiness. Reflective thinking is ... troublesome because ... it involves willingness to endure a condition of mental unrest and disturbance. Reflective thinking ... means judgment suspended during further inquiry; ... [the] most important factor ... consists in acquiring the attitude of suspended conclusion, and in mastering the various methods of searching for new materials to corroborate or to refute the first suggestions that occur. (Dewey 1910)

Of course, the question for us is how true this century-old conclusion about decision making is in today's business world. The answer is that shortcuts in the process; "uncritical" and non-"reflective" thinking; and an inability or unwillingness to "maintain the state of doubt and to carry on systematic and protracted inquiry" are all too common in the world of business. Those are the reasons why ensuring effective strategic decision making forms the second interlocking component of building our preview of the proposed transformation.

Reinforcing Dewey's assertions, a recent article in the *Harvard Business Review* assessed "four myths about the manager's job that do not bear up under careful scrutiny of the facts" (Table 2.3). As the article's research concludes, managers are not given to reflective thinking, but chose to rely heavily on their intellect, recall, and experience when processing and formulating decisions relative to significant volumes of information they have received. The consequence is that in order to accommodate this

Table 2.3 Four myths of management

Myth	Fact
1. The manager is a reflective, systematic planner.	Managers' activities are characterized by "brevity, variety, and discontinuity" and are "strongly oriented to action and dislike reflective activities."
2. The effective manager has no regular duties to perform that distract from strategic considerations.	Managerial work involves performing a range of interpersonal roles (e.g., hosting clients); informational roles (e.g., processing information, e-mails); decisional roles (committing resources, initiating new processes/programs).
3. The senior manager needs aggregated information, which a formal management information system best provides.	Managers favor assimilating, analyzing, and reaching decisions based on information received directly (e.g., from meetings) as opposed to reading documents, reviewing computer-generated analyses, or assessing analytics.
4. Management is, or at least is quickly becoming, a science and a profession.	As with executives of a 100 years ago, today's executive seeks information by word of mouth. Contemporary business may be technology driven, but procedures used to make decisions are essentially the same as those used by leadership's nineteenth-century counterparts.

challenge, strategic decision making becomes reliant on "analogous thinking" (Mintzberg 1990).

In taking an approach built upon analogy, managers assume there is sufficient correspondence between a previous situation with which they are familiar or have had experience and the current challenge they face; accordingly, they tend to conclude that the same attributes that contributed to the original venture's success will translate directly into success of the proposed new enterprise. The risk in making such an assumption is that without the proper discipline and depth of analysis, what on the surface may be assumed to be a quick, ready, and easy solution may, in fact, prove itself to be a demonstration of uncritical thinking—the potential selection of an inapplicable, inappropriate, costly, and unsuccessful path forward.

In his analysis of decision making, Dewey had recognized and warned against this casual, uncritical use of analogical thinking. As he described, the mind "demands some principle of continuity" that can induce "forces" within us that can ascribe "fantastic and mythological explanations" to supply the "missing links" between suppositions and well-constructed analyses.

> We have not yet made the acquaintance of the most harmful feature of the empirical method. Mental inertia, laziness, unjustifiable conservatism are its probable accompaniments.... Wherever the chief dependence in forming inferences is upon the conjunctions observed in past experience, failures to agree with the usual order are slurred over, cases of successful confirmation are exaggerated. (Dewey 1910)

Unless the analysis is thorough—with similarities and dissimilarities between the previous experience and the proposed application carefully dissected—opportunity exists (and probability suggests) that what might have been assumed to be an easy solution will, in fact, turn out to be an inappropriate solution. If, for example, we think back to the Introduction of this book, we might recollect that whereas the Wright brothers were the first successfully to fly a powered, heavier-than-air plane, Samuel Langley would have preceded them had it not been for faulty analogous thinking: Although steam engines had a successful history of powering trains, their size and weight made them poor choices to power Langley's Aerodrome.

Nonetheless, this potential weakness in analogous thinking should not suggest that it is invalid for our purposes of drafting a reasonable preview of the transformation. To the contrary, as noted in a second, recent *Harvard Business Review* article, "Analogical reasoning makes enormously efficient use of the information and mental processing power that strategy makers have." In comparison, as the article goes on to explain,

> processing a great deal of raw data is very challenging, particularly if there are many intertwined choices that span functional and product boundaries. The mental demands of deduction can easily outstrip the bounds of human reasoning that psychologists have identified in numerous experiments. (Gavetti and Rivkin 2005)

It is precisely for this reason, the need for an immediate and facile means of synthesizing a great deal of information into a preview of the transformation, why analogical thinking is valuable at this juncture of the process.

However, as just noted, to use analogous thinking effectively as a foundation for the actual implementation of the transformation, corporate leaders and managers must be cognizant of the "pitfalls of analogy." In addition to guarding against accepting an analogy without challenging the applicability of its similarities and the magnitude of the dissimilarities with the proposed solution, managers must be aware of two associated inclinations that can contribute to faulty, uncritical thinking: (1) anchoring—the eagerness to accept an analogy without sufficient evaluation, often resulting from the strength with which the analogy is introduced or by deference to the individual or the office held by the individual who proposes the analogy, and (2) confirmation bias—the inclination of decision makers to seek out information that substantiates their conclusion accompanied by an overt or unintentional tendency to ignore information that is contradictory or challenges the efficacy of the analogy. As the *Harvard Business Review* article just cited concludes,

> Together, anchoring and the confirmation bias suggest real problems for strategists who rely on analogies. Having adopted an analogy, perhaps a superficial one, strategy makers will tend to look for evidence that it is legitimate, not evidence that it is invalid.

Yet, as was noted, as opposed to a costly, time-consuming course of research that may jeopardize responding to the urgency of the need for the transformation, analogous thinking provides the capability to streamline and expedite development of a credible preview of the transformation. The goal, simply stated, is to use analogical thinking wisely—to ensure the analysis represents solid critical thinking unhindered by inadvertent anchoring or confirmation biases.

As such, to ensure the appropriateness of and an expedient use of analogical thinking when considering a transformation, the company leadership needs to develop and agree upon sufficiently detailed answers to five questions:

1. What similarities are we basing the analogy on? Are they foundational attributes (key concepts) that contributed directly and

significantly to the success of the venture to which the transformed company is being compared? Are they immediately applicable and implementable?

2. What are the dissimilarities between the referenced example and the proposed transformation? Are these differences significant enough to potentially undermine or limit success of the transformation?

3. Have the discussions of the reference condition been thorough? Has open discussion brought to bear the collective knowledge, expertise, and experience of all members of the leadership team or has the analogy been accepted without thorough examination and challenge?

4. Where opinions about the applicability of the analogy have digressed, have the discussions been candid and thorough enough to ensure potential issues are not dismissed owing to anchoring or confirmation biases (i.e., deference to a more senior individual)?

5. Once an analogy has been dissected and the correspondences deemed appropriate, has there been any independent validation of the leaderships' conclusions relative to initiating the transformation?

Once the answers to the questions that frame these first two interlocking pieces have been completed, this evolving preview of the transformation is then complemented by the third interlocked component. Whereas corporate positioning represents a straightforward assessment of the company's current and proposed status, and the introduction of disciplined analogical reasoning complements it with a preliminary understanding of the anticipated attributes and risks associated with the transformed company, the final interlocked component—defining the reasonable customer— puts the picture in more acute focus. This third component examines the most fundamental bedrock of the transformation and the most substantial measure of the venture's likelihood of creating a profitable and sustainable business—a projection of the value customers will perceive of the transformed company's proposed new products and/or services.

Component 3: The Reasonable Customer Analysis

By far the most substantial element of any transformation is to answer the questions whether the transformed company will produce products and/or services that successfully provide value for its customers, and whether that value will be significant enough to differentiate the company from its competitors to create customer loyalty and corporate sustainability. When an accurate understanding of the targeted customer base is added to the detail provided by analysis of the first two interlocking components, company leadership has an effective assessment of the transformation's potential challenges and rewards.

Phrased in the language of contemporary management science, having completed a thorough analysis utilizing all three of our interlocking features, leadership will have constructed answers to all five principal elements that Peter Drucker, a theorist often referred to as the founder of modern management, identified as the predicates of a successful business strategy:

1. What is our business?
2. Who is the customer?
3. What is value to the customer?
4. What will our business be?
5. What should it be? (Webster 2009)

As with other aspects of generating a preview of the transformation, the activities associated with customer analysis may appear very simple and straightforward. Yet, as with defining the positioning of the transformed company and making prudent and defensible decisions about the strategies to deliver the transformed company, conclusions derived require a systematic and disciplined approach if the answer is to be credible and accurate. So, too, does it apply to the process for identifying future customers and their expectations.

As example, let's reconsider the case with which we began this chapter: the NHS's records centralization project. The end goals of that initiative should have made evident the four sets of customers or beneficiaries:

1. Patients: Primary expectation is the ability to check their personal test results from home and book follow-up appointments as might be warranted.
2. Health care professionals: Primary expectations are the ability to gain ready access to fast, reliable, and accurate information about patients, and to access local and national health-care-related information systems.

3. NHS managers and planners: Primary expectations are the ability to monitor overall program performance and the ability to better assign and evaluate use of resources.
4. The public: Primary expectation is the ability to judge the performance of local hospitals and other health care providers.

The next step (Dewey's problem definition step) should have been for the system developers more exactly to define these expectations so as to provide concrete direction for the programmers and designers. Recognizing that each of these four customer groupings represents a very large and diverse population, it would be impossible to reach out to every customer to delineate and accommodate each person's specific expectations. Gathering feedback through extensive engagement with all communities would be far too daunting an undertaking—especially in these early planning stages of such a project and given the constricted project schedule. In contrast, it would not be difficult to surmise the general range of expectations that might be encountered within each group.

Considering just the first customer grouping, patients, there are likely to be those who want a gold-standard system: instantaneous access to any tests or visit results; extensive analyses of each test; analytics that put the newest results in context of any previous related tests; a very exact prognosis; comparisons of treatment options; and prescheduled follow-up appointments. At the other end of the spectrum of this customer grouping are likely users who simply want to have access to a brief, nontechnical summary of test results with an ability to schedule a follow-up appointment if so desired.

Although conceivably both ends of the spectrum and every potential position in between could be accommodated where there are no time, financial, or technical constraints associated with the system being developed, realistically, practical design decisions need to be made regarding all inputs and outputs. Ultimately, the specifications for the system need to consider how to reconcile the vast range of expectations with such considerations as the sophistication of available technology, personnel resources available for system implementation, and, of course, budget and schedule restraints.

And yet, whether the system was being designed to meet the exacting standards of the most demanding customer or to satisfy the expectations of a significantly less demanding user, it should be capable of satisfying what Peter Drucker considered the essence of customer value: "What the customer buys and considers value is never a product. It is always utility, that is, what a product or a service does for the customer" (Webster 2009). The means of defining what expectations need to be accommodated, what utility to be provided to customers, needs to begin not with either polar end of the spectrum but, rather, with an understanding of what "a reasonable customer" would consider value.

Years ago when first confronted during a transformation with this apparent dilemma of needing to reconcile with a range of poorly defined, seemingly irreconcilable sets of expectations, we came up with our simple methodology: Begin the design analysis by determining what a reasonable customer would expect. Then, based upon introducing the relevant considerations—for example, market opportunities, corporate vision, and existing constraints such as schedules and budget—all expectations (e.g., quality, breadth, production volumes, marketing, and distribution of the perceived product line) can be scaled up or down; in so doing, products and services can be effectively aligned with the goals of the transformed company, the expectations of the leadership team, and any absolute bounding conditions.

The example we use most often to explain the concept of the reasonable customer is to consider the activity of buying a car. Allowing for the fact that there are a growing number of companies offering online car sales, let's assume the customer in our example prefers purchasing vehicles at a dealer car lot. So, here's the question, what does the reasonable customer in this situation expect? Clearly, the purchaser is expecting a quality vehicle at a good price. The customer also expects that the actual process of purchasing the vehicle will be straightforward, comfortable, and can be accommodated in a reasonable amount of time.

Having done most of the work before going to the car lot—selecting the model, interior and exterior colors, accessories, and price range—a reasonable customer would anticipate that the only action at the dealership other than completing the paperwork should be the need to test-drive the model to determine whether the vehicle performed up to his or her standards and expectations. It is also reasonable to assume that the paperwork will not require a great deal of time or inconvenience.

However, that is not necessarily the experience the buyer has. What should be a relatively undemanding implementation step—the process of completing the sale—as many of us have experienced—often stretches into an activity that seems unnecessarily and annoyingly longer than what is perceived as warranted. Rather than a quick set of signatures, the process for purchasing the vehicle becomes a multi-hour activity, often requiring engagement with several dealership employees.

What the reasonable customer had anticipated—a quick completion of the sale—is not what occurs. In having failed to meet the customer's expectations—even if not verbalized by the customer—the dealership has failed.

The process was neither reasonable nor did it represent the level of "utility" Drucker identified as the foundation of customer value. Although pleased with the vehicle purchased, the customer is likely displeased with the experience, a response that may make the customer less inclined to want to re-enact the activity with the dealership any time soon.

In contrast, recognizing what a reasonable customer is expecting should form the basis for the dealership to consider redesign of the purchase process. In this instance better aligning the experience with the customer's expectations should be extremely easy being that all facets of that experience are under control of the dealership. The challenge is not a technical one but, rather, a reflection of the degree to which the company designs practices from a customer-oriented perspective. Considering the two factors of interest to a reasonable customer in this illustration—convenience and value—the dealership might implement any number of changes.

For example, essential paperwork can be completed in the office while the customer takes the test-drive. Another example might be if customers, without the aid of a salesperson, were given access to an automated checklist of options and accessories that calculates their impact on total vehicle cost so as to allow customers to take their time, un-harried, in reaching decisions about which options are of interest and value to them. The enhancements, as just these two examples suggest, would not only positively transform the customer experience; they would differentiate the dealership from its competition and, at the same time, possibly reduce the dealership's administrative and labor costs.

Given these added insights into assessing expectations of reasonable customers, let's momentarily return to the NHS's "contracting fiasco." Given the government's intention to deliver a comprehensive program in three years and within a finite budget, one can define the extent of utility and sophistication of the centralization effort. In each of the four customer brackets, the government, in conjunction with limited representation from that group, should have started with the idea of "what's reasonable?" What can we, in seeking to deliver the new NHS system, accomplish that satisfies the intended goals of the project and meets the expectations of a "reasonable customer"? Do the sets of expectations from the four customer groups collectively provide an implementable set of capabilities that add utility for the customer—value being determined in terms of functionality, convenience, reliability, performance, efficiency, and accessibility?

Once those expectations had been established, then the question should have become "can we do better given the schedule and funding constraints?" Can we implement those expectations or are they beyond our capacity to deliver? This discussion, often iterative, would conclude when the expectations for each of the four customer brackets had been established, reconciled against each other to ensure their balance and their cohesion into an integrated program—a system that adds value and utility, is feasible to implement within the pre-established constraints, and is sustainable over time.

The last of these two attributes—implementable and sustainable—would inevitably have led to another set of questions about delivery of the system. In particular, one of the foremost issues—the breadth of anticipated subcontracting—would have needed to be considered. What mechanisms and controls were in place to ensure subcontracted scopes of work were discrete, concrete, fixed, would integrate successfully, and were appropriately constructed so as to provide the best value to the government—that is, effectively delineating use of fixed price, time and material, and cost plus subcontracts. By not having taken this step of looking at the delivery process, as we noted, the NHS unintentionally contributed to subcontracts whose scopes of work were poorly defined, overlapping, contradictory, and distributed across an overly large network of corporations.

Had the reasonable customer analysis been applied to the internal customers as well, the various disciplines and agencies critical to effective subcontracting would have been integrated through the development of a transformed subcontracting process. Discussion and expectations would have centered on such fundamentals and expertise needed to design a process that attends to a range of critical factors:

- The length of time it takes to prepare and approve each subcontract
- The length of time to award the subcontract, including validating qualifications and capabilities of prospective vendors

- Ensuring the scope of each subcontract is absolutely clear along with expected timelines for all deliverables
- The means and junctures for performance monitoring/auditing and periodic progress reviews are commensurate with the complexity, cost, and schedule of each subcontract.
- The payment mechanism is capable of handling the anticipated number and frequency of invoices.
- Penalties are delineated for poor quality of work and for schedule or cost overruns.

This component of the reasonable customer analysis would thereby translate into a program that ensures all the necessary disciplines are engaged at the appropriate times in the subcontracting process. Figure 2.3 is a matrix we developed in an experience paralleling this particular aspect of the NHS project, wherein our project also required significant attention to ensuring the integrity of the subcontracting process.

Conclusion

Making certain that your company's transformation initiative is on a course that is aligned with your vision, is feasible, and will lead to an implementable and sustainable outcome is best and most appropriately accomplished before launching into the actual implementation. The goal is to take full

Responsible Organization	PROCESS ACTIVITY					
	PRE-PROCUREMENT PLANNING	VENDOR QUALIFICATION	SUBCONTRACT DEVELOPMENT & REVIEW	SUBCONTRACT APPROVAL & AWARD	SUBCONTRACTOR OVERSIGHT	INVOICE PROCESSING & PAYMENT
Requester / Requisitioner						
Project Controls						
Engineering						
Quality Assurance						
Subcontract Oversight						
Safety						
Finance						
Property Management						
Training						
Warehouse						

Figure 2.3 Subcontract development and oversight

advantage of the experience and perspectives of the leadership team while making certain not to mistake "uncritical" evaluations for well-reasoned analyses; the goal is to define with reasonable accuracy what the company's transformation is going to produce. In short, avoiding the pitfalls that occur when plans are not defined, expectations are unclear, and funding and implementation schedules are unreasonable is best accomplished by developing as robust and clear-sighted as possible a preview of the road ahead.

In our experience, creating this preview—creating the opportunity to assess your ideas, vision, and implementation—is best accomplished by completing four steps:

1. Determine the impetus for the enterprise transformation and the projected positioning of the transformed company within the marketplace of choice
2. Conduct a disciplined assessment based on using the combined leadership experience, expertise, and intuition using analogous thinking to allow the assessment to be completed in a timely, cost-effective fashion
3. Determine the value and utility you expect to create for your customers using a reasonable customer analysis and then scaling the expectation to align with your vision
4. Construct a basic model of the principal impacts and process changes within the organization to deliver the new line of products or services

At the end of the day, you can control and chart the path to a successful transformation. Using the tools—engaging in practices like analogous thinking to identify and evaluate potential transformational opportunities—complemented by an intense, unflinching commitment to adding value for your customer, you can avoid the characteristics of the failings of transformation attempts such as that of the NHS.

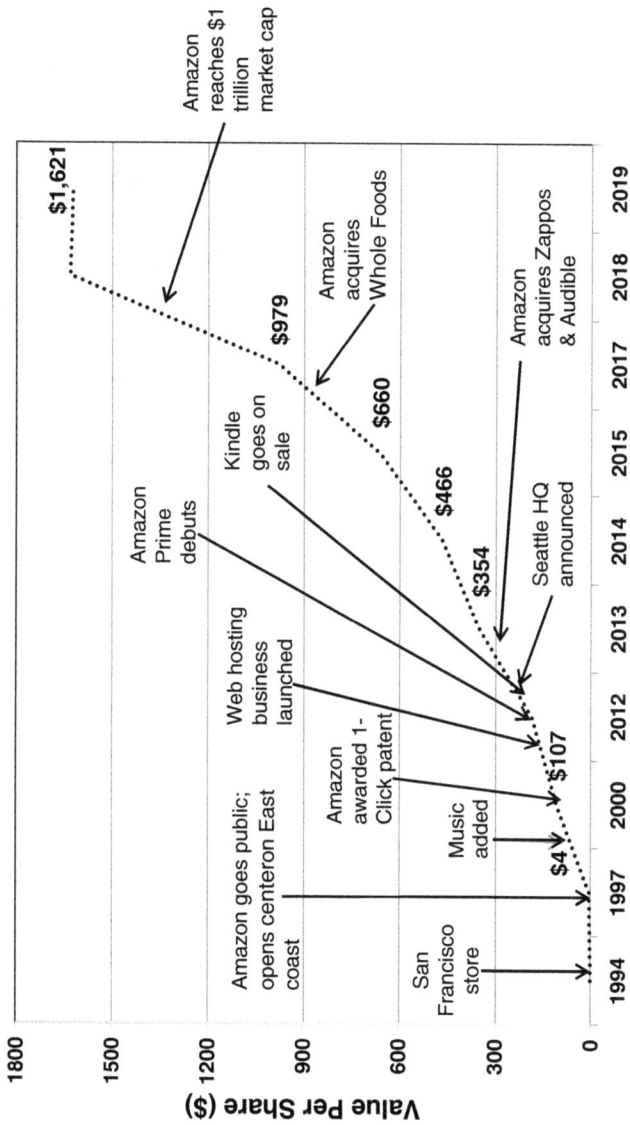

Figure 2.4 *Amazon's history of successful transformations*

The predicates of effective transformation planning inherent in our three interlocking components are the same underlying principles that have made corporations like Amazon leaders in envisioning the future and routinely transforming themselves in anticipation of how to increase utility and provide value for their customers (Figure 2.4).

Using these tools and techniques will provide a clear image of the road to a successful enterprise-wide transformation. Effectively previewing and anticipating opportunities and challenges—examining the planned positioning of your company; ensuring critical, reflective thinking in designing your path forward; and concentrating on increasing utility and customer value—will substantially increase the likelihood of the company's success and will prepare all facets of the company—from the boardroom to the working level—for the actual transformation process detailed in the next chapters.

CHAPTER 3

The Mechanics
of Transformation—
A Leadership Perspective

Simplicity is the ultimate sophistication.
—Attributed to Leonardo DaVinci

A Bit of Perspective

Largely as a function of a concern over the influx of illegal narcotics (and secondarily to control illegal immigration), in 1997, the U.S. Immigration and Naturalization Service (INS) deployed the first of several attempts to introduce technology as a primary means of border surveillance: the Integrated Surveillance Intelligence System (ISIS).

ISIS was a system of sensors and cameras: radar to detect objects, motion sensors, infrared sensors to detect heat, seismic detectors to monitor for vibration, and magnetic sensors to detect metals. In addition, the system relied on remotely operated surveillance cameras to capture descriptions of people and vehicles. Any activity detected triggered an alarm, detail was processed through the project's Intelligent Computer-Assisted Detection (ICAD) database, and Border Patrol personnel were then dispatched. As of October 2005, 11,200 sensors had been deployed (10,500 of which were operational) along with 255 cameras; however, in the 7+ years following the project's authorization, the equipment deployed only succeeded in providing surveillance of approximately 4 percent of the combined U.S. northern and southern borders (GAO 2002).

With issuance of the Homeland Security Act of 2002 and the establishment of the Department of Homeland Security (DHS), technologically based border surveillance underwent its first significant change. ISIS was replaced with the America's Shield Initiative (ASI), whose aim was two-fold: (1) address ISIS capability limitations, and (2) support the department's anti-terrorism mission. In so doing, the intent was to enhance and integrate technology accompanied by addition of tools that would analyze the collected information and then generate decision support information to assist Border Patrol agents. As example, new capabilities, such as enabling agents to send and receive information while in the field, were to be coupled with interoperability among DHS and law enforcement agencies, and by customized software designed to produce a common operating picture—a uniform presentation of activities within specific areas along the border.

A few years later, with passage by Congress of HR 6061, The Secure Fence Act of 2006, DHS replaced ASI with a much more technologically ambitious project to secure the southern border. Opting only to study the necessity/feasibility/and economic impact of establishing "operational control" over the northern border, the Act placed clear strategic attention on the southern border.

In addition to enhanced "physical infrastructure," the Act authorized funding for "systematic surveillance … through more effective use of personnel and technology, such as unmanned aerial vehicles, ground-based sensors, satellites, radar coverage, and cameras." With this mandate, in November 2005 the DHS commenced the Southern Border Initiative Network (SBInet)—often euphemistically referred to as the "virtual fence."

In the years following fiscal year 2006, DHS received roughly $4.4 billion in appropriations for SBInet, representing approximately $2.5 billion for physical fencing and related infrastructure, $1.5 billion for virtual fencing and related infrastructure (e.g., towers where cameras were to be mounted), and approximately $300 million for program management. Originally forecast to cost approximately $7 billion to provide surveillance of 2,000 mi. of border, a pilot program in Arizona—the only area where the surveillance capabilities were actually deployed—cost about $1 billion to build the system across just 53 mi. of the state's border. Prohibitive costs and schedule delays were exacerbated by technical problems and issues with hardware operability: for example, instability of cameras during adverse weather conditions, signal loss from the cameras, and issues with sensitivity and alignment of the radar.

Consistently dissatisfied with the performance of the program, in January 2010, DHS ordered an assessment of the project, followed in March by a freeze on project funding. In May 2010, the General Accounting Office (GAO 2010a) issued a scathing report. The report's conclusion offered the following summation:

> Given ... the magnitude of the initial investment ... coupled with the fact that the scope of the initial system's capabilities and areas of deployment have continued to shrink, the program is fraught with risk and uncertainty. As a result, the time is now for DHS to thoughtfully reconsider its proposed SBInet solution.

Given the project's history and the weaknesses confirmed in the GAO report, in January 2011, Janet Napolitano, the DHS Secretary, ended the project. In terminating the project, which had already spent more than $1 billion, Secretary Napolitano restated the conclusions cited by the GAO, declaring that SBInet "does not meet current standards for viability and cost effectiveness." Acknowledging the project's failure to deliver on expectations, the Secretary further noted that the virtual fence "cannot meet its original objective of providing a single, integrated border-security technology solution" (GAO 2006, 2008, 2009, 2010b).

Unlike the failure of the NHS system discussed in Chapter 2, which was a consequence of such features as poorly defined expectations, arbitrary timelines, unwillingness to recognize when a course correction might be warranted, SBInet and its predecessor attempts at building a virtual fence did not exhibit these same weaknesses. Rather, at inception, SBInet had all the earmarks of what should have been a successful project: a capable, experienced contractor; reliance on off-the-shelf, commercially available surveillance equipment; clearly delineated expectations; and a commonly shared understanding among DHS and its stakeholders as to what would have constituted project success.

Unfortunately, what SBInet did not have was a mature, conscientiously applied project management or Earned Value Management System (EVMS)—the means by which to measure progress against cost and schedule commitments and thereby identify risks such as potential cost overruns and schedule delays early enough to allow management to take actions to avoid or minimize adverse impacts.

In summary, the GAO faulted SBInet for a catalog of project management weaknesses:

- A reliable schedule for completing work had not been developed.
- Cost-effectiveness had not been demonstrated.
- Life cycle costs had not been reliably estimated.
- Expected mission benefits had not been adequately defined.
- Life cycle management activities had not been consistently performed.
- Requirements had not been adequately developed and managed.
- System and operational requirements were poorly defined and traceability had not been maintained to determine if requirements were being met.
- Key risks had not been effectively managed and disclosed.
- Risk management had not been fully implemented.
- Baselines were incomplete, unrealistic, and not validated.
- Project scope and complexity had been underestimated.

Managing the Transformation: Primary Principles

At the most basic level, effective management of a transformation project is contingent on maintaining a conscientious and disciplined adherence to a dozen key principles:

- Clearly defined lines of accountability for all aspects of the work
- Sound, disciplined, upfront project planning
- Well-defined and documented project requirements
- Well-defined and managed project scope
- Reliable and accurate cost estimates
- Stable funding profiles that support and are aligned with cost estimates
- Sufficient numbers of skilled and trained personnel
- Sufficiently sophisticated management systems: for example, risk management, change control, and contract management
- A robust risk management program
- Early and continued engagement of all functions and disciplines central to successful delivery of the transformation; for example, safety, quality control, human resources

- Effective and sustained communication among management, the workforce, and stakeholders
- Utilization of periodic peer reviews to assess performance opportunities and issues

Yet, as Secretary Napolitano noted as regards to implementing SBInet, no system can provide a one-size-fits-all solution; rather, the elements must be tailored to reflect the complexity of the transformation, the expectations (e.g., cost and schedule), and the unique circumstances that accompany every transformation (e.g., different local laws, different regulations, unique community relations). Although some transformations are large enough (generally above $50 million) to warrant an array of sophisticated program management tools and software, others can be accommodated with more simple techniques that embed the principles of sound project management.

Fundamentally, the principles of earned value rely on four key integrated practices:

- Maintaining control of project scope
- Maintaining effective cost management
- Maintaining a realistic schedule
- Relying on a robust risk management program to identify, characterize, and track disposition of potential adverse situations

In other words, successful transformations require a robust commitment to the basics of performance management (Figure 3.1).

Tracing EVMS to its roots makes evident that to demonstrate these four practices does not necessarily demand complex analyses and sophisticated software attended by staffs of dozens of estimators, schedulers, consultants, and cost account managers. Originally predicated on the work of Frank and Lillian Galbreath (discussed in our Introduction), whose motion studies introduced the concept of "earned time," earned value did not always translate into the complex systems most often described in contemporary management literature. Rather, the practice, as we and our colleagues used it in our professional careers beginning many years ago, relied on a much simpler and more immediately direct means of introducing and adhering to the four key attributes just enumerated.

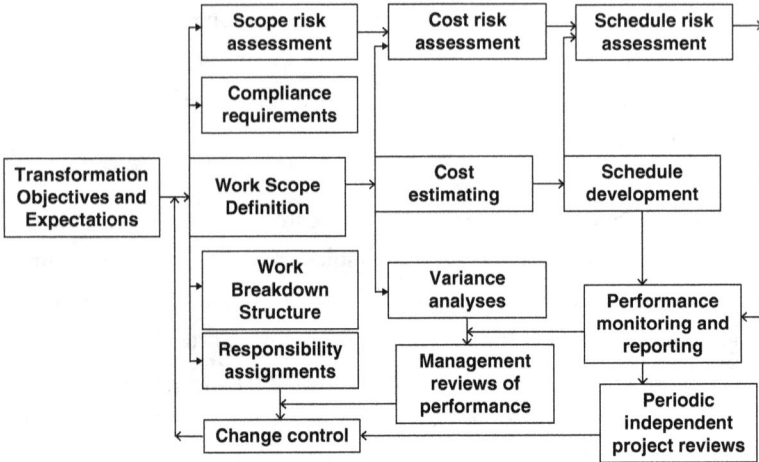

Figure 3.1 Sequence for managing transformation projects

Cost/Schedule Control System Criteria (C/SCSC), the forerunner of contemporary performance management systems, encapsulated in 35 criteria essentially all the requirements for a successful project management program. (The 35 criteria are summarized in Figure 3.2.) Largely a suite of commonsense expectations, the breadth and reasonableness of C/SCSC was effectively articulated in a 1984 "information pamphlet" issued by the Department of Energy (DOE). As the primer detailed, the 35 criteria in a C/SCSC system were grouped into five major categories. Generally, these five groupings delineate the following requirements:

1. Organization: The system is expected to provide clear definition of the overall effort, with a work breakdown structure serving as a framework for displaying subdivisions of effort. Additionally, integration must be established among the planning, scheduling, budgeting, work authorizing, and cost accumulating subsystems.

2. Planning and budgeting: All authorized work must be planned, scheduled, budgeted, and authorized within the system. Establishment of a performance measurement baseline is the key requirement of this section.

3. Accounting: Costs of completed work must be accumulated from the levels at which costs are initially recorded up through the project level.

The 35 Cost / Schedule Control System Criteria			
ORGANIZATION 1. Define all authorized Work 2. Identify Responsibilities 3. Integrate the work breakdown structure and organization with the planning, scheduling, budgeting, work authorization, and cost accumulation systems 4. Identify the managerial positions responsible for controlling indirect costs 5. Provide for integration of the contract work breakdown structure with the organizational structure *PLANNING AND BUDGETING* 6. Schedule all authorized work 7. Identify all products, milestones, and performance goals 8. Establish and maintain a time-phased budget baseline at the cost account level 9. Establish budgets for all authorized work, identifying separate cost elements (labor material, etc 10. Identify discrete, short-span work packages or identify the far-term effort for budget and planning purposes	11. Provide that the sum of all work package budgets plus planning packages within cost account equals the cost account budget 12. Identify relation-ships of budgets or standards in underlying work authorization systems to budgets 13. Identify and control level of effort activity by time-phased budgets established for this purpose for work packages 14. Establish overhead budgets for the total costs of each significant organizational component 15. Identify management reserves and undistributed budget 16. Provide that the contract target cost plus the estimated cost of authorized but unpriced work is reconciled with the total project cost *ACCOUNTING* 17. Record direct costs on an applied or other acceptable basis	18. Summarize direct costs from cost accounts into the work breakdown structure 19. Summarize direct costs from the cost accounts into the contractor's functional organizational elements 20. Record all indirect costs that will be allocated to the contract. 21. Identify the basis for allocating the cost of apportioned effort 22. Identify unit costs, equivalent unit costs, or lot costs, as applicable 23. The accounting system will provide for: accurate cost accumulation; determination of price and cost variances; cost performance measurement; and full accountability for all material purchased 24. Identify at the cost account level: a. Budgeted cost of work scheduled: budgeted cost of work performed and variances *ANALYSIS* 25. Identify cost data on a monthly basis: budgeted cost of work scheduled; budgeted cost of work performed and applied; and variances 26. Summarize the data elements and associated variances to the appropriate reporting level	27. Identify significant differences between planned and actual schedule accomplishment 28. Identify managerial actions taken as a result of criteria 24 - 27 29. Based on performance to date, develop revised estimates of cost at completion *REVISIONS AND ACCESS TO DATA* 30. Incorporate contractual changes in budgets and schedules in a timely manner 31. Reconcile original budgets for those elements of the work breakdown structure with current performance measurement budgets 32. Prohibit retroactive changes to records pertaining to work performed 33. Prevent revisions to the contract budget base 34. Document internally, changes to the performance measurement baseline 35. Provide open access to the information and documents demonstrating compliance with the cost/schedule control system criteria.

Figure 3.2 C/SCSC requirements summary

4. Analysis: Comparisons of actual versus planned performance are required. Thresholds for variance analyses must be established to avoid excess effort which may otherwise result from analyzing insignificant variances.

5. Revisions and access to data: A meaningful performance measurement baseline must be maintained complemented by processes that include reconciliation of estimated costs at completion and funding (DOE 1984).

A basic depiction of the system should make evident that the predicates of performance management are essentially little more than the introduction of commonsense oversight tools—tools that should not be intimidating or beyond the capacity of even the smallest of companies (Figure 3.3). It is not a matter of how sophisticated the system is but, rather, the continued attention to cost and schedule performance—a sustained, thoroughly thought out, carefully reasoned, and well-disciplined approach to ensure the transformation is proceeding in keeping with the intended costs and schedules.

As a practical, personal validation that using our tools and strategies will deliver a capability that provides for the essential project management controls, we might briefly recollect our first experience using our tools in the transformation of a company. Our first encounter with transforming a company occurred back in the mid-1980s. In that instance, as we prepared to implement the tools we had developed to manage the transformation of a mid-size company, we were assailed by certain stakeholders who very self-assuredly protested that accounting for cost and schedule performance on essentially a real-time basis could not be achieved without reliance on a mainframe computer.

In response, using a whiteboard we illustrated the inputs, outputs, and interfaces of all the components that collectively represented the equivalent

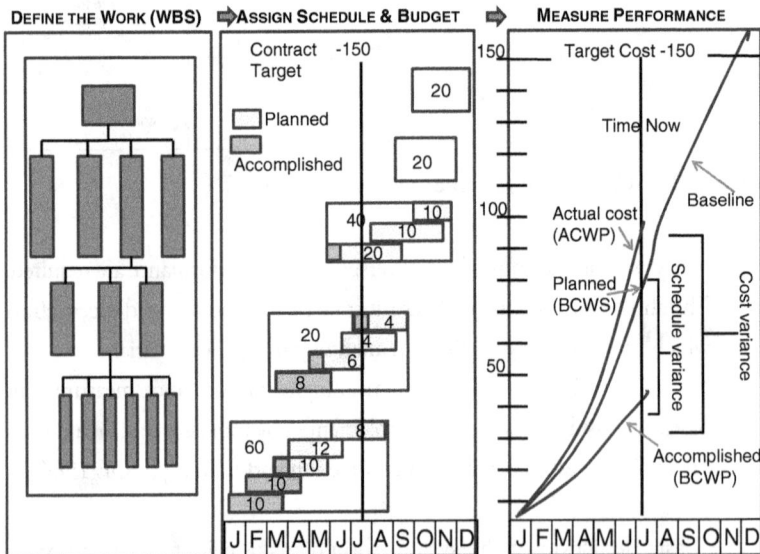

Figure 3.3 Summary depiction of a project management system

of implementing C/SCSC. We then overlaid our tools and methodology, demonstrating their correspondence to the 35 C/SCSC criteria.

Having demonstrated the ability to construct a tailored management system, we then proceeded to implement the program on a series of personal computers (computers that, at the time, could likely not match the computing capability of today's tablets). The program, as implemented, not only supported successfully completing the transformation of the company, but also served as the performance management system used by the company for many years following startup.

As one might expect given our foundational concept of the reasonable customer as examined in Chapter 2, whether employing a full-blown performance management system—that is, an EVMS—or our streamlined and tailored approach, the key factor in determining success is recognizing and fittingly addressing the two different and significant perspectives: (1) the expectations and mechanics of monitoring scope, cost, schedule, and risk as evidenced at levels of upper management responsible for developing and maintaining the strategic vision, and (2) the relationship to those same four components of effective program management as perceived and implemented by the workers in the company who own and are counted upon to realign functions and services to meet that vision.

To highlight the significant differences inherent in the two perspectives, we are going to examine each of the two orientations separately. Given that the senior management perspective is the one more commonly associated with contemporary EVMS literature and doctrine, we will begin there. The view at the functional level will be the focus of Chapter 4.

We will allow for the fact that companies employing a full cadre of project control specialists already have the software, hardware, and personnel resources they require for delivering all the sophisticated capabilities of a comprehensive EVMS. In contrast, our attention here is not to restate the mechanics of analyzing schedule floats, using precedence diagramming, or representing time-phased formats as would require that level of sophistication and investment; rather, our goal is to explain the underlying principles and provide the tools, techniques, and strategies we have developed over the years that have allowed us—and will allow company leadership of any size company—to have full control of and confidence in steering the course of the company's transformation.

Managing the Transformation: The View from the Top

To gather a complete picture of the project and the elements by which to manage it, management will first need to assemble its thoughts about what the transformation is about and how the execution of the transformation is intended to proceed. Sometimes a document that is used for this purpose is referred to as a project execution plan (PEP). It establishes and integrates the policies and procedures for managing and controlling project planning, initiation, definition, and execution; it is an accurate and precise summary of how the project is to be accomplished, resource requirements, technical considerations, risk management, configuration management, and roles and responsibilities.

Table 3.1 summarizes the contents most commonly included in a comprehensive PEP. As evident, not all sections will be applicable or relevant to all transformation projects. Only the sections that apply to the transformation need to be fleshed out; likewise, the level of detail in each section should be commensurate with the need to ensure that all project participants share the same sense of what it entails to be successful. Once this summary overview of all the attributes of the transformation have

Table 3.1 Project execution plan checklist

Section Heading	Basic Description	Required (Yes or No)
Introduction	Purpose and organization of the plan	
Background	Brief history/background and statement of major objectives	
Rationale	Reasons why the transformation is being undertaken	
Description	Vision, major assumptions expectations, requirements, scope, and stakeholders	
Management structure	Overall management organization, including roles and responsibilities of key team members	
Budget	Time-phased explanation of funding	
Staffing	Personnel needs by area of technical specialty	
Standards	Applicable standards, laws, regulations	

Table 3.1 Continued

Section Heading	Basic Description	Required (Yes or No)
Time-sensitive activities	Long-lead procurements, permits, and other activities that drive the schedule for completing the transformation	
Scope baseline	Technical and programmatic descriptions derived from requirements, planning, reference and design documents	
Schedule baseline	Schedules sufficiently developed to support understanding of planning and execution sequences	
Cost baseline	Total cost to complete transformation supported by a work breakdown structure (WBS)	
Risks	Cost and schedule risks and uncertainties with explanation of how these have been determined	
Risk management	Policies and practices for identifying, characterizing, quantifying, and tracking risks	
Change control	Processes and procedures for executing baseline changes, change control thresholds, and approval authorities	
Integration management	Activities and deliverables due from other projects, parent companies, and stakeholders	
Communication management	Practices, methods, frequencies for communicating with stakeholders, the workforce, and interested parties	
Reporting	Formal reporting, including content, distribution, frequency, and approval requirements	
Reviews	Peer and independent reviews, audits, and assessments	
Key support functions	Business, technical, and management functions essential to deliver major milestones, e.g., quality control, engineering	
Project controls	The process to be used to capture, monitor, and analyze performance data along with explanation of how the data is integrated into decision making	
Transition to new company	Principal components delineating how transition and project commissioning will be accomplished, including provision for any training or procedures that may be needed	

been recorded, the challenge turns to executing the transformation and, in particular, providing attention to and leadership decisions regarding the chief project management elements: scope, cost, schedule, and risk management.

Managing the Scope

As noted in Table 3.1, gaining a sufficiently sophisticated understanding of total cost for the transformation requires a comprehensive picture of the scope (the work that needs to be done) and how the elements of the scope are interrelated. This picture is accomplished most effectively by developing a WBS that extends down to a level of detail that provides a practical and implementable understanding of the planning needed and the specific means for executing the work.

Generally, this level of specificity will entail a WBS that provides several tiers of successively more detailed delineation of the scope, each tier of which is commonly referred to as a "level." A WBS for a relatively complex scope of work, as shown in Figure 3.4, might include details descending down through Level 6 or 7, with the interrelationships expressed as a series of reflexively assigned number designations. A simple project, in comparison, might rely on a single tier (Level 1) for conducting planning.

Generic WBS Structure
WBS 1.0 Summary level: Used by senior management in tracking the transformation at its highest levels
WBS 1.1 Principal Work Component: Large scopes of work as may be assigned to the next level down of management
WBS 1.1.1 Specific Supporting Unit: A set of inter-related functions assigned to an individual manager
WBS 1.1.1.1 Group Function: Assigned to a specific function, e.g., engineering
WBS 1.1.1.1.1 Cost Account: Sub-function level at which costs are tracked
WBS 1.1.1.1.1.1 Specific Scope of work: Inter-related activities as might be associated with a single deliverable
WBS 1.1.1.1.1.1.1 Work Package / Planning Package: A single self-contained activity

Figure 3.4 Generic WBS structure

The individual levels, as noted, provide the framework for project planning, data collection, performance measurement, and reporting. They also provide the flexibility by which each team participating in the transformation can develop the appropriate level of planning, budget, and control. For example, while one component (e.g., records management, finance) that typically has periodic, routine activities (e.g., processing invoices) might only plan and report at the cost account level (Level 5), physical tasks associated with operations or engineering are likely to be planned at a higher level of detail (e.g., Level 6 or 7).

The simplest means of developing the WBS is by creating a depiction of the organization planned to accomplish the transformation. This approach, often referred to as an organization breakdown structure (OBS), is particularly suited for smaller-scale transformations (transformations of average size companies rather than large corporations) that can be effectively managed at a broader level of control. (Figure 3.5 offers an example of a WBS based upon an organizational structure.)

Once the organizational structure is built and before the actual work on transformation is initiated, a thorough understanding of each of the scope elements is required. The most effective means of accomplishing this end is to develop a WBS dictionary, a two-part document containing both a listing of all WBS elements and a definition of what the scope element entails. As with the WBS itself, the definition only needs to be detailed enough so that all managers, workers, and organizational units dependent upon one another have a common understanding of what activities are to be done and what constitutes completion of the WBS element. The reason for providing clarity on completion of the scope element is to avoid too narrow a definition as in the case when a simple WBS structure (two or three levels) is used or to avoid possible overlap among WBSs where significantly more specificity is provided (i.e., Level 6 and 7 detail).

For example, using the organization depicted in Figure 3.5, the teams responsible for factory retooling and equipment overhaul need to share precisely the same definition of overhaul work so as to ensure there is no confusion as regards precisely what equipment is scheduled to be removed and in what sequence. (Table 3.2 is an example of a WBS dictionary format and entry.)

TRANSFORMATION SERVICES LTD

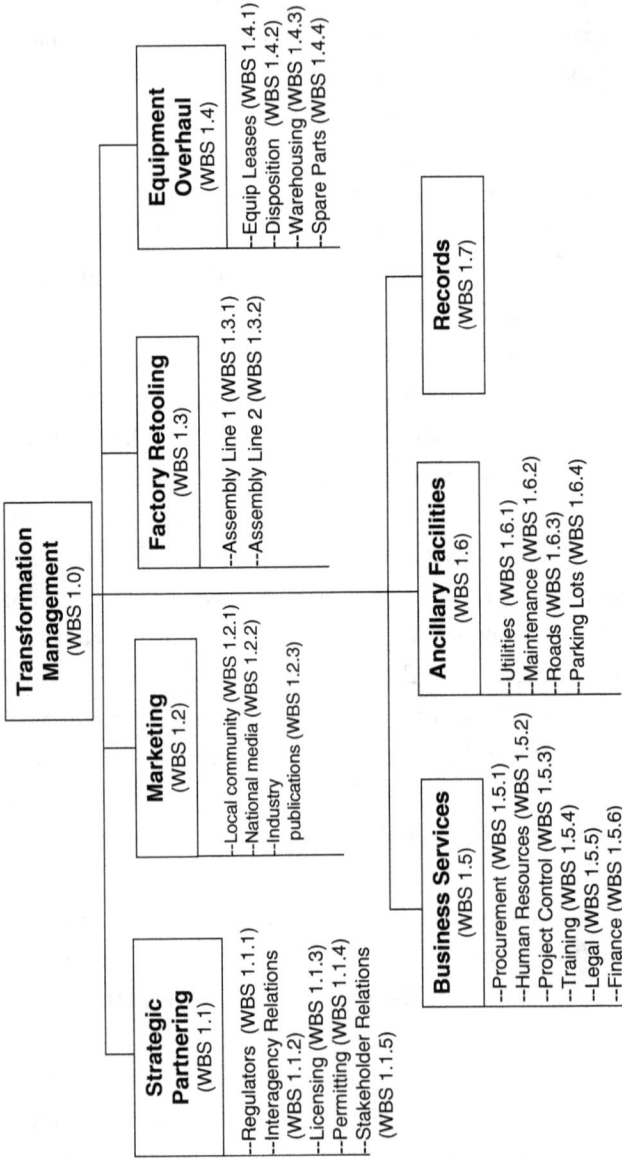

Transformation Management (WBS 1.0)

Strategic Partnering (WBS 1.1)
--Regulators (WBS 1.1.1)
--Interagency Relations (WBS 1.1.2)
--Licensing (WBS 1.1.3)
--Permitting (WBS 1.1.4)
--Stakeholder Relations (WBS 1.1.5)

Marketing (WBS 1.2)
--Local community (WBS 1.2.1)
--National media (WBS 1.2.2)
--Industry publications (WBS 1.2.3)

Factory Retooling (WBS 1.3)
--Assembly Line 1 (WBS 1.3.1)
--Assembly Line 2 (WBS 1.3.2)

Equipment Overhaul (WBS 1.4)
--Equip Leases (WBS 1.4.1)
--Disposition (WBS 1.4.2)
--Warehousing (WBS 1.4.3)
--Spare Parts (WBS 1.4.4)

Business Services (WBS 1.5)
--Procurement (WBS 1.5.1)
--Human Resources (WBS 1.5.2)
--Project Control (WBS 1.5.3)
--Training (WBS 1.5.4)
--Legal (WBS 1.5.5)
--Finance (WBS 1.5.6)

Ancillary Facilities (WBS 1.6)
--Utilities (WBS 1.6.1)
--Maintenance (WBS 1.6.2)
--Roads (WBS 1.6.3)
--Parking Lots (WBS 1.6.4)

Records (WBS 1.7)

Figure 3.5 Sample organizational breakdown structure

Table 3.2 Sample WBS dictionary entry

WBS Dictionary				
WBS Number	WBS Title	Primary Area of Scope	WBS Definition	WBS Owner
WBS 1.4.2	Equipment disposition	Equipment overhaul (WBS 1.4)	During the course of retooling Assembly Lines 1 and 2, several pieces of major equipment (current book values in excess of $10,000) such as conveyor systems and remotely operated articulating fabrication systems will need to be removed to clear areas for the new product manufacturing capabilities. WBS 1.4.2 is responsible for: (a) identifying salvageable equipment; (b) removal of items to designated staging areas; (c) completing and documenting disposition of each piece of equipment; and (d) transferring any funds collected from sales or auctions to management reserve.	J. Smith

Managing Cost

Estimating and monitoring costs is the most critical factor in being able to assess the health of the transformation project. The step that is most essential in this context is development of the cost estimate. Irrespective of the means by which the company collects costs during the transformation, the determination of whether or not the project is on course and going to complete consistent with the anticipated cost of the journey is conditional on two primary factors: (1) how good the cost estimate was when the project begins, and (2) how well aligned the cost and budget (the amount of funding allocated to the project as a whole as well as to the individual WBS elements) remain during the complete tenure of the project. Stated in slightly different terms, ultimately, to be reliable, a cost estimate should reflect four characteristics:

- Comprehensive
- Well documented
- Accurate
- Credible

"Comprehensive" is synonymous with "complete." The estimated cost should include all costs extending over the transformation's full duration: vision development, strategic planning, and execution; costs of design, development, subcontracts, equipment and material purchases; labor costs; and allowances to accommodate unforeseen events and risks that have a reasonable probability of occurring.

Documents and any other resources that might have been developed or referenced in the course of defining the vision and determining the definition of success should be consulted, for example, market studies, professional society publications, internal reports. Although the estimate does not necessarily have to delve into exhaustive detail, it should have sufficient detail so as to provide confidence that cost elements are neither omitted nor double counted. For instance, for a straightforward transformation only anticipated to last for a limited period of time, a simple estimate as shown in Table 3.3 might suffice.

"Well documented" means that as the transformation progresses and questions arise or adjustments are required, the company has sufficient documentation to allow it to understand how the numbers in the cost estimate were derived: the source and significance of the data used, the calculations performed, their results, and the rationale underlying the approach taken to developing the estimate. Essentially, the cost estimate is creating a trail, a means to trace back through the individual cost elements, the process, and the assumptions.

This capability is especially significant in transformations with high costs and long durations; it is not uncommon that circumstances (e.g., appreciable changes in the cost of materials) may require recalculating the estimates or validating that assumptions used in preparing

Table 3.3 Basic cost estimate for transformation

	Phase 1	**Phase 2**	
Labor			
Management	$112,280	$115,949	
Strategic partnering	$60,000	$40,991	
Marketing	$15,344	$35,850	
Factory retooling	$186,664	$254,630	
Equipment overhaul	$36,913	$20,673	
Business services	$141,676	$125,723	
Ancillary facilities	$28,365	$13,534	
Records	$12,905	$15,741	
Total Labor	$594,147	$623,091	$1,217,238
Other Direct Costs			
Insurance	$1,200	$1,200	
Equipment	$345,820	$265,820	
Subcontracts	$80,900	$48,700	
Travel	$12,837	$6,500	
Miscellaneous/Risk contingency	$11,718	$7,681	
Legal fees	$38,000	$0	
Total Other Costs	$490,475	$329,901	$820,376
Total Transformation Costs			$2,037,614

the estimate remain reasonable. As a component of maintaining a well-documented cost estimate, a record should be maintained that documents assumptions used and the basis and rationale for any revisions to the estimate. It is also good business practice to have the initial cost estimate and any substantive adjustments to the estimate independently reviewed by people who did not contribute to the estimate's development.

"Accurate" is a reflection of how realistic the estimate is. The cost estimate should not be overly conservative or overly optimistic; it should reflect most likely costs as they are known at the time. Because costs potentially change, for example, value of money, escalation, the estimate should be revisited and revised as necessary on a periodic basis to account for material changes in the program and actual cost experience gained during the transformation.

"Credible" is a function of whether the bases and assumptions are valid, for example, were there any limitations in the analysis that were introduced owing to uncertainty or biases inherent in the data or assumptions (e.g., allowances for anticipated rates of inflation). The point is that any risk and/or uncertainty inherent in the estimate should be assessed, the underlying assumptions examined, and the rationales and conclusions documented.

Most typically, cost data and cost performance are assessed on a monthly basis, with performance (comparison of projected versus actual costs for the period) assessed at both the function and at the project levels. As with development of the cost estimate, performance reporting can be detailed or can be simple just as long as it effectively assists leadership in determining, assessing, and remediating variances. (Figure 3.6 is a sample of a typical cost performance report (CPR) generated using a comprehensive EVMS that processes collected data through a series of analytical software.)

The important feature here, as we have mentioned, is not how sophisticated the reporting format is but whether the information is sufficiently packaged so as to allow management to arrive at judicious decisions regarding the continued path forward for the transformation. Consistent with the elements reported in a CPR, what the leadership needs to know are just two things: (1) costs and budgets for the current reporting period and the project to date; (2) variances between how much has been spent versus what was expected to have been spent, again as determined for both the current reporting period and the project to date.

Cost variance for the reporting period, in EVMS parlance, is expressed as the Budgeted Cost for Work Performed (the total value of all completed work) minus the Actual Cost of Work Performed (all incurred costs accounted for to date). Cost variance for the project as a whole (Variance at Completion) is expressed as the Budget at Completion (the total cost determined by the cost estimate) minus the Estimate at Completion (the amount spent to date plus the total additional budget needed to complete the project). Positive variances

COST PERFORMANCE REPORT

TRANSFORMATION SERVICES LTD

($ IN THOUSANDS)

DESCRIPTION		CURRENT PERIOD					INCEPTION TO DATE					AT COMPLETION		
		BUDGETED COST OF		ACTUAL COST OF WORK PERFORMED (ACWP)	VARIANCE		BUDGETED COST OF		ACWP	VARIANCE		BUDGET AT COMPLETION (BAC)	ESTIMATE AT COMPLETION (EAC)	VARIANCE AT COMPLETION (VAC)
WBS	TITLE	WORK SCHED (BCWS)	WORK PERF (BCWP)		SCHED	COST	BCWS	BCWP		SCHED	COST			
1.1	SP	4.5	4.7	6.1	0.2	(1.4)	12.6	13.3	16.2	0.7	(2.9)	21.0	23.4	(2.3)
1.2	MAR	3.7	4.1	3.5	0.4	0.6	9.7	11.2	7.9	1.5	3.3	17.5	16.1	1.4

Figure 3.6 Sample cost performance report

indicate that activities are costing less than expected; negative variances indicate activities are costing more than projected.

In either instance, whether a positive or negative variance, the important considerations are: (1) what information management needs to understand the factors and causes contributing to the variance, and (2) what information management needs in order to make deliberate, reasoned, and judicious decisions regarding the variance. Those reasons are why any variance needs to be accompanied by an analysis that includes a range of considerations:

- What caused the variance?
- Are the effects isolated or will they impact interrelated functions?
- Is the variance an anomaly or indicative of a trend?
- Does the variance require immediate attention and, if so, what actions need to be taken—when and by whom?
- Should adjustments be made to the current cost estimate and/or the estimate of completion?

The essential point is that not all variances are bad, but all variances need to be understood.

Managing Schedule

A reliable schedule provides a road map for systematic execution of a program; it provides the means to assess progress and a means to identify and take action in response to potential problems. To be effective, a schedule, like the cost estimate, should be complete, accurate, and credible: All activities should be identified on the schedule; the timelines for each activity should be consistent with the anticipated durations; and the time to complete activities should be reasonable. In effect, an effective schedule should satisfy the five elements cited in the schedule checklist below (Table 3.4).

Depending on the complexity of the transformation, schedules may be very simple or very detailed; only a single-level schedule may be sufficient or several schedules may need to be developed—each successive schedule providing a greater level of specificity, for example, project level, function level, task level. Figure 3.7 is an example of a simple milestone schedule

Table 3.4 Schedule checklist

Criterion	Effectively Demonstrated		Adjustments Needed
	Yes	No	
1. All activities from all WBS elements accounted for?			
2. Sequences among tasks within a major activity are correct and logical?			
3. Relationships and sequences between major activities are correct and logical?			
4. If appropriate, have resources been assigned to activities reasonable?			
5. Are proposed durations for activities achievable?			

that might accompany the short-term project suggested by the organization chart (Figure 3.5) and the cost estimate (Table 3.3) discussed previously.

This chart form—derived as are most schedule formats from Gantt Charts developed during World War I by Henry Gantt as a means to provide better information regarding the movement of supplies—is a very efficient means of portraying the anticipated flow of the project. It is at once easy to generate, easy to understand, and easy to monitor. As with cost estimates, it serves as a ready contributor to senior management decision making: The numbers and types of milestones to be included on the schedule can be defined by management determining the intermediate accomplishments of greatest significance, and schedule variances (acceleration or slippage) in completion of milestones are immediately identifiable.

In the example below, the major activity lines are divided according to the responsibilities assigned to the different organization units. As shown, there is supposed independence among the work of the organizations. Additional detail could have been added to show the interdependencies: Predecessor-to-successor relationships could have been included to indicate when the work of one organization fed into or represented a precursor to the start of an activity within another organization.

In the case where a transformation project entails a multi-tier set of schedules, there are a few added expectations: (1) vertical traceability that

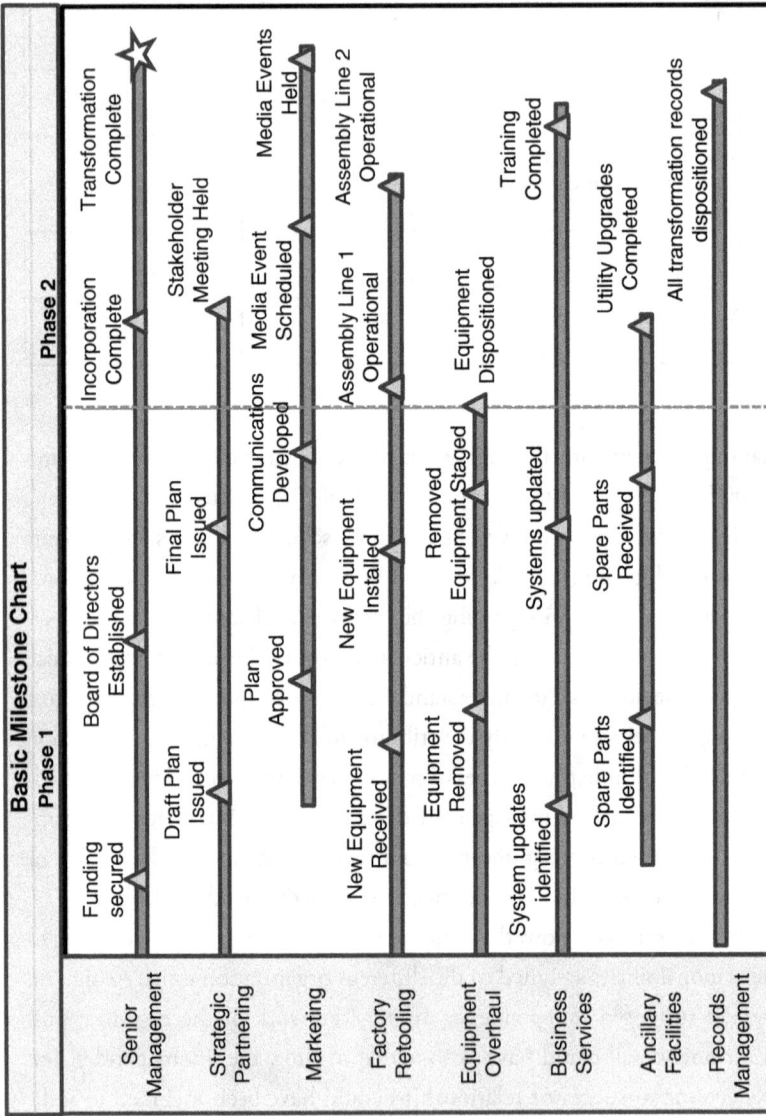

Basic Milestone Chart

	Phase 1	Phase 2

Senior Management — Funding secured · Board of Directors Established · Incorporation Complete · Transformation Complete

Strategic Partnering — Draft Plan Issued · Final Plan Issued · Stakeholder Meeting Held

Marketing — Plan Approved · Communications Developed · Media Event Scheduled · Media Events Held

Factory Retooling — New Equipment Received · New Equipment Installed · Assembly Line 1 Operational · Assembly Line 2 Operational

Equipment Overhaul — Equipment Removed · Removed Equipment Staged · Equipment Dispositioned

Business Services — System updates identified · Systems updated

Ancillary Facilities — Spare Parts Identified · Spare Parts Received · Utility Upgrades Completed · Training Completed

Records Management — All transformation records dispositioned

Figure 3.7 Sample milestone chart

allows a user to move between the schedules and readily understand how the work at one schedule level effects or is effected by the work cited on a different level. Maintaining this coordination is benefitted by a sufficiently robust WBS that announces relationships among related tasks and scopes of work. (2) Historical traceability that provides the configuration control between revisions of the schedules and between the schedules and other project documentation such as the PEP. In this regard, changes to the project schedules, as with changes to the cost estimate, should be rigorously controlled and well documented to ensure changes are effectively implemented and fully understood.

Managing Risk

Risk—like cost, scope, and schedule—has to be continually monitored and updated throughout the duration of the transformation. To ensure a complete, accurate, and current understanding of risks, the program needs to consider appropriately tailored approaches to each of five elements:

- Developing a plan to manage risk
- Identifying risks
- Assessing and quantifying risks
- Developing action plans to mitigate potential adverse effects consequent to the risks and
- Tracking the implementation and success of risk mitigation measures

Risks can be identified in two ways: (1) using checklists that focus attention on commonly experienced risk areas, and/or (2) evaluating on a function-by-function basis what risks might be associated with each WBS or element of the entire project scope. Whether one method or the other is used (or both in conjunction with each other, thereby amplifying the likelihood that all significant risks are captured), the uncertainties are identified by screening and reviewing the scope, schedules, and cost estimates along with their assumptions. (As illustration of the two methods, Table 3.5 provides a checklist of commonly encountered risks and uncertainties; Figure 3.8 suggests how the risks might have been determined by having managers examine their respective areas of responsibility.)

Table 3.5 Checklist of commonly experienced risks

Risk Category	Specific Risk	Risks Effectively Addressed in Performance Execution Plan		Further Action Assigned to
		Yes	No	
Economic environment	Economy stable?			
	Changes in competition anticipated?			
Planning	Expectations/requirements identified?			
	Expectations/requirements realistic?			
	Expectations/requirements complete?			
	Constraints effectively identified (e.g., funding, regulatory)?			
	Assumptions valid and confirmed?			
	Any potential delays owing to regulatory approvals, permits?			
	Adequate planning documentation available, e.g., PEP, drawings, schedules, procedures?			
Supply chain	Subcontractor availability confirmed?			
	Resources available?			

Category	Question							
	Prices stable?							
	Subcontract types appropriate (e.g., fixed price)?							
	Subcontract requirements clear and appropriate (i.e., tailored to the work)?							
	Incentives (e.g., safety) established for subcontractors?							
Technical	Appropriate safety/security/quality controls in place?							
	Physical and cyber security controls sufficient?							
	Needed technology is stable and available?							
	Sufficient number/timing of independent reviews scheduled?							
Budget	Complete/sufficient funding determined and secured?							
	Cost estimate reliable, thorough, accurate, documented, and credible?							
Staffing	Staffing commensurate with project size, complexity, training locally available?							
	Potential problems with recruitment/relocation/housing?							

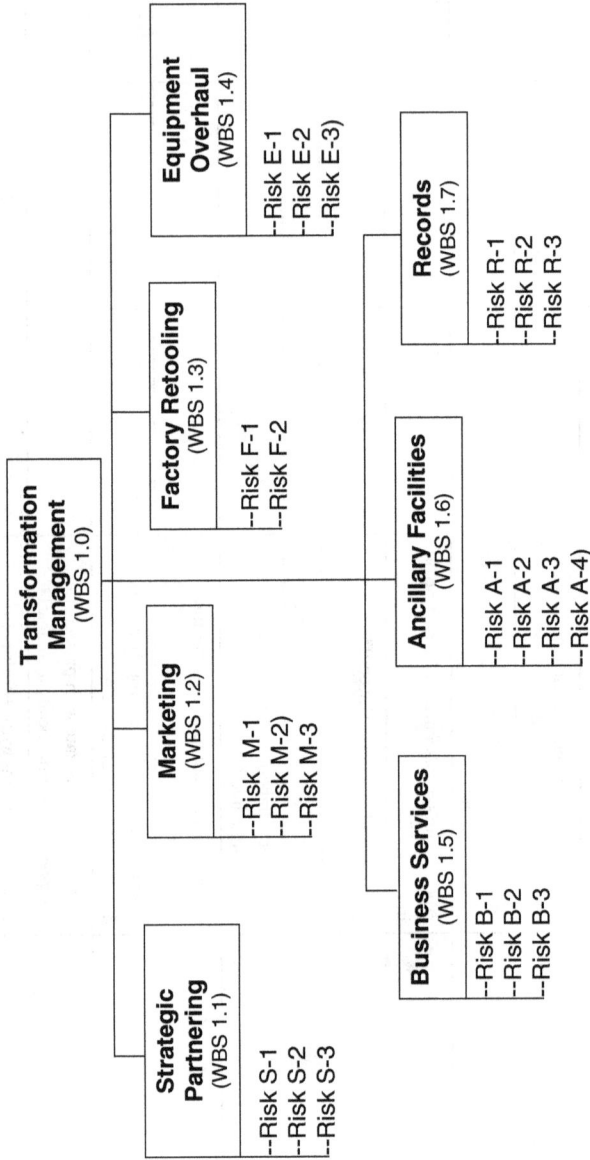

Figure 3.8 Risks and uncertainties identified by function

For each uncertainty identified during the risk screening, an owner is assigned who forecasts the likelihood of an unacceptable outcome occurring. To assess severity of consequences, owners forecast what might go wrong and what effect those occurrences might have on scope, cost, and schedule. To the extent feasible, the consequences are quantified. For example, if a new production technique is being applied that is lower cost with a shorter schedule to implement than had been used in development of the cost estimate and schedule, the impacts may be readily derived. In contrast, predicting probability of a particular event occurring is more judgmental and represents the owner's best judgment.

To reflect the two variables (consequence and probability), as shown in Figure 3.9, probabilities are ranked in terms of ranges of percentages representing likelihood of occurrence; severity (the impact on cost and schedule) is delineated as adjectives suggestive of consequence: the impact is anticipated to be negligible, marginal, major, critical, or a crisis.

Risk Categorization						
		Consequence				
		Negligible	Marginal	Major	Critical	Crisis
	Cost	Minimal consequence; cost increase can be absorbed	Slight increase in cost; small added difficulty in meeting expectations / cost estimate	Significant increase in cost and serious difficulty in meeting expectations / cost estimate	Cost estimate not achievable; additional funding may need to be secured	Complete disruption and possible need to stop and/or terminate transformation; scope adjustment needed, at minimum
	Schedule	Minimal consequence; effect on schedule can be absorbed	Limited added difficulty in maintaining schedule; slippage can be made up	Significant adverse impact on schedule; schedule will have to be revised	Milestones are not achievable; schedule pushed out far enough to effect numerous factors (e.g., permits)	Complete disruption and possible need to stop and/or terminate transformation; schedule redrafting needed, at minimum
Probability	Very high (90%+)	Low	Moderate	High	High	High
	High (70 – 89%)	Low	Moderate	Moderate	High	High
	Moderate (35 – 69%)	Low	Low	Moderate	Moderate	High
	Low (10 - 34%)	Low	Low	Low	Moderate	Moderate
	Very Low (<10%)	Low	Low	Low	Low	Moderate

Figure 3.9 Basic ranking system for transformation project risks

Having once identified the risks, the goal—as with developing the cost estimate and the periodic review of schedules—is to integrate the information into the decision-making process throughout the entire period of the transformation. Typically, to support the routine monitoring of the risks identified, the most effective strategy is to create what is often referred to as a risk register. In addition to the scores determined for the consequence and probability, the register is used to record and track the effect of assigned mitigating actions. These actions, as with the assessment of cost and schedule, need to be periodically monitored and adjusted as necessary until such time as the risk is either eliminated or fails to occur. (Table 3.6 is a sample of an entry in a risk register.)

Conclusion

The essential elements of effectively guiding the course of a transformation are, as we have shown, a matter of common sense. Whether using a comprehensive EVMS, C/SCSC, a set of index cards, or the tools we have just discussed, successful transformation project management is a matter of paying keen, disciplined attention to the quality and control of the project scope, costs, schedule, and risks. Armed with the understanding you now have, with knowledge of the principal considerations that need to be heeded; the tool set by which to identify, monitor, and direct the course of the transformation; and the clear vision of what constitutes success, company leadership has the preparation and capability to conduct an effective transformation.

Synthesizing the essence of this discussion on the mechanics of the transformation process, the efforts required of company leadership can be expressed as a simple, 20-question checklist—a checklist that aggregates the attributes of retaining a sustained focus on scope, cost, schedule, and risk into a compressed statement of what needs to be tracked, managed, and communicated to all involved in the transformation—management, workers, stakeholders (Table 3.7).

The challenge of effectively leading a transformation project, as Table 3.7 suggests, all along, has not been whether the company had possession of sufficient technology to proceed, but, rather, did the company leadership have the right focus, a firm commitment, and a knowledgeable

Table 3.6 Sample risk register entry

Risk Number	WBS Number	Description	Rankings		Assigned to	Proposed Actions	Status
			Consequence	Probability			
F-1	1.3	Machinery from EYZ company critical to the retooling effort is delayed or placed on back order.	Major	Moderate	C. Shaw	1. Contracts working directly with EYZ, including addition of penalties for late delivery 2. Secondary schedules being developed that allow work-arounds 3. Quality control personnel assigned at EYZ to expedite receipt and acceptance testing	Contracts expected to be modified and signed in advance of next program review Work-around schedules expected to be available for review 6/14

Table 3.7 Managing the transformation: The essentials

Performance Criterion	Sufficiently Developed and Documented		What Needs to Be Done
	Yes	No	
Scope			
Is total scope understood?			
Has an effective WBS structure been implemented?			
Is there a complete WBS dictionary?			
Cost			
Is the cost estimate comprehensive?			
Is the cost estimate well documented?			
Is the cost estimate accurate?			
Is the cost estimate credible?			
Schedule			
Are all activities from all WBS elements accounted for?			
Are the sequences among tasks correct and logical?			
Have resources been assigned to activities?			

Schedule			
Have appropriate milestones been identified?			
Are durations assigned to tasks reasonable?			
Risks			
Have risks associated with the economic environment been identified, assessed, and mitigating actions determined?			
Have risks associated with the planning been identified, assessed, and mitigating actions determined?			
Have risks associated with the supply chain been identified, assessed, and mitigating actions determined?			
Have risks associated with the technical components of the transformation been identified, assessed, and mitigating actions determined?			
Have risks associated with the budget been identified, assessed, and mitigating actions determined?			
Have risks associated with staffing been identified, assessed, and mitigating actions determined?			
Control			
Has a systemic approach been established for periodically assessing whether adjustments are needed as regards scope, cost, schedule, and risk?			
Are there other factors essential to the success of your transformation you need to assess and routinely monitor?			

appreciation of how to apply a tailored set of implementation tools and mechanics commensurate with the anticipated complexity of the transformation initiative.

With this arsenal of tools available to you, moving forward with the transformation, in its simplest articulation, is chiefly a matter of understanding that, as the quotation attributed to DaVinci submits, "Simplicity is the ultimate sophistication."

CHAPTER 4

The Mechanics of Transformation: A View from the Shop Floor

The best way to predict your future is to create it.

—Abraham Lincoln

In August 2011, a large piece of concrete smashed through the windshield of a car being driven in Montreal, Canada. Accustomed as they were to similar events, the people in Montreal assumed the problem was part of the continuing deterioration of the city's infrastructure. Seeking to calm the public, the city's mayor offered a rather curious pronouncement: "I want to assure the people of Montreal: the rock that caused this incident has nothing to do with the structure [the Champlain Bridge]."

The fact that the concrete had been tossed by someone rather than had broken off from the body of one of Canada's busiest bridges on its own and had fallen onto the car below seemed of little comfort. As the news report quoting the mayor asserted, "it's hard to blame even the most paranoid residents for assuming the contrary. It's raining concrete in Montreal" (Gohier 2011). The seriousness of the city's problem had been most effectively captured by a roadside advertisement admonishing motorists to, "Say Your Prayers," as they approached the Champlain Bridge (The Canadian Press 2011).

The previous month a 50-ft long, 25-ton mass of concrete had fallen onto an expressway; in 2006, five people died and six more were seriously injured when an overpass collapsed onto cars travelling below; in 2000, eight heavy concrete beams fell from another overpass, killing one person and injuring two others. The city's response each time had been to initiate emergency repairs on local bridges and ramps along with repairs on some of the city's busiest interchanges, including one in particular that, for a number of years, had been periodically shedding large pieces of its construction unto the surfaces below. Overwhelmed by this continuing threat of falling concrete, more than 50 percent of people surveyed in Montreal at the time indicated they were "scared" to drive under an overpass, on a bridge, or through a tunnel (Gohier 2011).

Perhaps foremost in contributing to issues with the infrastructure's performance was reliance on cost as a predominant factor driving engineering and construction decisions. Stating the matter succinctly, one study concluded, the "problem boils down to the ill-advised design choices ... used in the rush to build up Montreal ahead of Expo '67 and the 1976 Olympics" (Gohier 2011). Or, as stated in a report issued shortly after the 2011 event: the infrastructure, rather than with a focus on safety, had been "designed rapidly and constructed with a view to efficiency, economy and speed of construction" (Perreaux 2013).

Recounting the implications of a cost-based decision model, a 2009 engineering report had previously suggested sections of the bridge's structure were in such a severe state of deterioration that a partial or complete collapse of the span could not be ruled out. That conclusion was subsequently validated when in November 2013 a crack was found in a critical part of the bridge's superstructure, necessitating immediate, emergency—yet, again, temporary—bridge reinforcement.

Basing decisions on cost had led to irresolvable engineering issues. Rather than following the original proposed design using steel girders for the entire span across the St. Lawrence River, a less expensive design using concrete reinforced by high-tension cables was selected. The design, as noted in an engineering assessment, integrated the bridge's components in a complex network of steel and concrete that made replacing a beam "difficult, if not impossible" (Perreaux 2013). Moreover, one cost-saving measure in the design was actually directly contributing to shortening the bridge's working lifespan: Because of the potential danger from ice accumulation during winter, routine salting was required; yet the design provided no conduit to remove the salt, which, when allowed to remain on component surfaces, attacked the concrete as well as the steel rebar used in girders, pylons, and other bridge components.

A feasibility study later in 2011 sealed the bridge's fate. The report indicated basic maintenance of the bridge would cost $18 million to $25 million per year, maintenance that would not, in fact, result in any improvement of the actual structure. Rather, the study indicated a replacement bridge was the most practical and sustainable option (as opposed to further bridge repair or carving a tunnel beneath the St. Lawrence River). With little other choice, Canada moved forward with construction of a new bridge (Perreaux 2013).

Almost 8 years after the 2011 event that triggered the final decisions to replace the Champlain Bridge, work on the replacement bridge—the Samuel De Champlain Bridge—was complete. In July 2018, the new bridge—proposed just 2 months after the 2011 concrete event and requiring 8 million work hours at a cost of approximately $4.5 billion—was opened for traffic. Shortly thereafter, demolition began on the old bridge at a projected cost of $400 million.

As would be expected at the completion of one of Canada's largest reconstruction projects, the new bridge was greeted with great fanfare and national sense of accomplishment. At the ceremonies opening the new bridge, Canada's Federal Infrastructure Minister not only lauded the new bridge, but also acknowledged an important lesson to be learned: "If the past has taught us anything, it is certainly the need to build sustainable, modern and quality infrastructure for all future generations" (The Canadian Press 2019).

Yet, the Minister may have considered one other important lesson that had been learned the hard way: It is not sufficient that all the individual components of a project are working well; the ultimate success of any project is contingent on both individual performance and the coordination among all organizations and functions. What constitutes a project success is the collective achievement not individual successes, a conclusion that is particularly challenging when engaged in lengthy, complex, multifaceted projects or transformations, encompassing the work of multiple players.

Although the replacement bridge was proceeding on course, not all had gone well with the project as a whole. Three overpasses built after 2013—one an $11-million structure built in 2015—were torn down in 2016 owing to the fact that their designs were incompatible with the Champlain Bridge replacement project. Around the time the 2015 overpass was completed, a consortium called the Signature on the Saint Lawrence (SSL) was chosen to build the new Champlain Bridge. As a spokesman for SSL recounted, "By the time we did our design, their work was finishing and we realized that we couldn't reuse these overpasses."

Two major issues consequent to a lack of coordination and cooperation precluded the overpasses' use: (1) they had been built with only two lanes but would be connecting to a section of the highway leading to the bridge designed to have three lanes; (2) the overpasses were built on incorrect angles, making proper alignment with the adjoining highway impossible (CBC News 2016). As SSL noted, the overpass couldn't be salvaged: "It was impossible for us to use them because they were not aligned properly with the new configuration of the corridor" (CTV News.ca Staff 2016).

Underpinning the need to replace the three new, costly overpasses was a lack of coordination among the many voices engaged in the project's design and construction decisions—decisions affecting both the overpasses and the replacement bridge. As one structural engineer opined, "You try as much as possible to anticipate some of the over-all design criteria, but it's not always possible because there are a lot of stakeholders that are involved, criterias [sic] are dynamic and they change" (CTV News 2016).

Upon learning of the $11-million error associated with the A-15 over-pass, an astonished Montreal mayor vowed to "look into" the matter. Motorists (the customers, as it were, for the project) were somewhat less forgiving. As one individual exclaimed, "I don't understand the struc-tural engineers; they could have foreseen this before. Look what they've caused—instead of doing one work at a time we're stuck going around the city. It doesn't make sense anymore" (LeClair 2016).

The message from the Champlain Bridge project is immediately ap-plicable to working through the many moving parts associated with con-ducting a transformation project: The process has to be systematically orchestrated, issues brought immediately to the forefront, and all the players and organizations kept informed, interconnected with each other, and knowledgeable of the progress and decisions of their colleagues.

Coordination and Cooperation

Teamwork, coordination, and cooperation—promoted by active communication—are the elements that translate into a successful transformation project. As was demonstrated in the Champlain Bridge replacement project, lack of coordination and cooperation contribute to four major hurdles that can also adversely affect the success of transformation projects: delays, redundancy, unavailability of critical information, and lack of commitment and innovation.

Delays translate into ineffectiveness and inefficiency; the consequences are felt in the damaged working relationships among the organizations expected to deliver the transformation and with stakeholders, customers, and oversight organizations that are expecting peak performance, adherence to schedules, and cost efficiency. Redundancy, as considered in the context of both LEAN manufacturing and Six Sigma, is one of the principal weaknesses in a poor performing organization. It represents a loss of time and money without any commensurate benefit or value. Information represents the lifeblood of the project: having information that is accessible, thorough, and accurate is critical in allowing each organization and subpart of the project to proceed with confidence that alignment among the functions is being maintained. Lastly, progress is a direct function of the organization's willingness and eagerness to accept and promote innovation, to challenge embedded or outdated protocols, and to try new approaches, methods, techniques, and tools.

Critical to making the tools we are about to discuss work for you is recognition that at their core is the commitment to fostering coordination, cooperation, and communication. The two-fold goal is (1) success of each individual attribute of the transformation project, but, ultimately, (2) an interlinked, interwoven collection of successes that translate into and equal (if not surpass) the anticipated expectations that were set for the transformation by the company leadership at the outset of the project.

From this perspective, the tools and the process we are about to describe are intended to provide the greatest likelihood of success of the transformation project (Figure 4.1).

Coordination Continuum

Limited Interaction

Regular Exchanges

Joint decision-making

Minimum Likelihood of Transformation Success

Continuum of Coordination

Strong Likelihood of Transformation Success

Unilateral Action

Limited Cooperation

Routine Collaboration

Integrated Activities

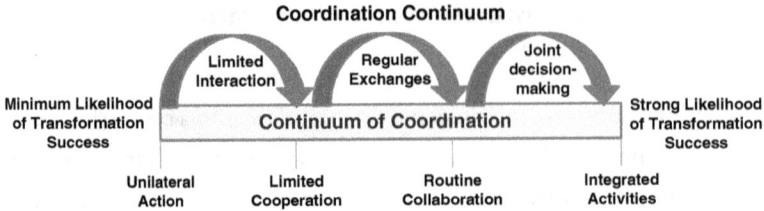

Figure 4.1 A basic coordination continuum for fostering project success

Each organization and each team member should have an explicit understanding of the roles, responsibilities, and authority that they as a team and as team members share. The sense of absolute team ownership is crucial, an ownership that recognizes that the leadership has entrusted the team with the company's future. To this end, the tools rely on and are designed to amplify three key factors that foster consistent, purposeful, and effective cooperation and coordination:

1. Clearly established team goals: Particularly on lengthy and complex transformations, teams must be able to see and validate progress. Near-term goals, supported by metrics, provide a basis for maintaining a tangible perception of how the team is doing and how that progress can be communicated to other teams and to company leadership. Incentivizing these intermediate goals is a powerful means of enhancing the camaraderie among team members and creating a sense of pride, value, and accomplishment.

2. Encouragement of creative thinking: Team members should recognize leadership's support in emboldening them to challenge the status quo, to look for and engage in discussions about new, novel, and innovative ways to achieve the team's goals and milestones. As appropriate, the team needs to consider introducing techniques—such as LEAN manufacturing—to trigger creative thinking. As with meeting team goals, incentivize innovation—reward teams (as a collective unit) for accelerating schedules, achieving cost savings, and better serving the needs of both internal and external customers.

3. Leverage team resources: One of the keys to successful transformations is benefitting from the talents and capabilities of every team member. To do this, leadership needs to create a discipline of collective decision making in which all team members are participants (Field 2014).

As depicted in Figure 4.2, enhanced cooperation and coordination are directly correlated with the effectiveness and thoroughness of communication—a condition that is true for both communication between organizations and communication within a single working team. If the team is consisting of people who are not familiar with one another's skills, experience, and capabilities, use team-building exercises early on to build team spirit and better to position the team to take full advantage of the team's resources.

Figure 4.2 The relationship among communication, coordination, and cooperation

The Workings of the Transformation

In the preceding chapter we examined the mechanics of completing the transformation project from the perspective of the company leadership. At this point, we need to examine the perspective of the workers actually delivering the transformation. To provide a thorough appreciation of the activities, we will partition this discussion into four sections:

- Getting started: A look at the initial steps of engaging the workforce
- Working with the teams: The process used to identify and characterize the activities and recommendations for completing the transformation project

- Pulling it all together: Examining how the tools and techniques fit together from the perspective of a single transformation team
- Getting feedback from the company leadership: The process of getting suggestions and authorizations to proceed with transformation actions and team recommendations

Getting Started

Placing the workforce in a position to proceed with transformation is contingent on three principal activities:

- Communicating expectations
- Establishing incentives
- Clarifying the path forward

Communicating Expectations

As was discussed in Chapters 2 and 3, the leadership will have already gone through various exercises and activities to establish precisely what the vision is of the transformed company. The important thing about having a concrete vision is the readiness to communicate it to those who need to support it—primarily the workforce.

Communicating the vision and expectations for the workforce can be addressed in a variety of ways. Most often there are letters or e-mails sent by the senior leadership to the workforce expressing what is being done, why, and what role the workers are to play. Yet, a narrative form is not the only means of engaging the workforce.

As example, Figure 4.3 is an approach to communicating the plan. In this figure, the inner circle provides, in relative terms, the amount of effort, resource, and costs anticipated for each of four components of the transformation project; outside the circle is a list of major actions and accomplishments needed that, collectively, translate into the transformation. Viewing this type of graphic, employees can gather very quickly and easily what is going to be taking place and, given their current jobs, can also readily ascertain the activities in which they are likely to be engaged.

GOAL: TRANSFORM THE COMPANY

"Rebranding / Repositioning / Reinvigorating"

Relocate business services
Centralize warehouse operations
Lease new facilities for
Assembly Line C

Reduce
Operational Costs

Retool Assembly Lines A& B
Implement automated processes
Integrate warehousing and
maintenance

Reduce aging
facility
infrastructure
costs

Change
marketing
strategy

Right-size
Overhead
functions

Start new ad campaign
Rebrand company
Focus on new customer base

Subcontract finance
Implement
enterprise-wide business
systems

Shapes Indicate Relative Percentages of Transformation Costs

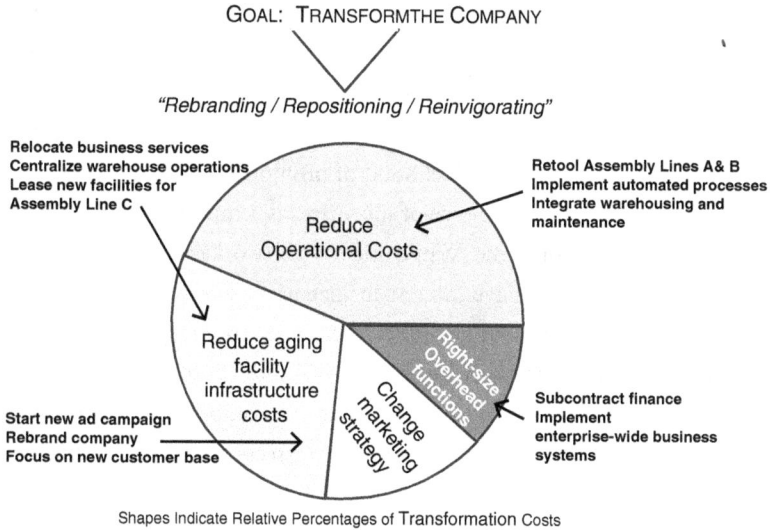

Figure 4.3 Communicating the transformation vision

Establishing Incentives

Although a matter of individual circumstances, we have found that providing incentives can both increase enthusiasm for the transformation and promote local ownership of the elements by the workforce. Coupling an incentive, an item of value, with a specific goal provides strong motivation to succeed. Stated differently, amplifying application of skills and resources through motivation equates to improved performance. The key to creating a powerful incentive program relies on a seven-step process.

1. Determine transformation goals: Understanding the goals allows leadership to reach two decisions: (a) what do you want to incentivize, and (b) what amount of incentive can be made available. Having already established what needs to be accomplished, leadership can consider whether such factors as schedule, cost, innovation, etc. are the most substantial contributors to the transformation's success. In each instance, the goals to be used in the incentive program need to be specific, tangible, and achievable. The workers' enthusiasm for the program will be a direct consequence of whether or not they believe the incentives are substantial and likely to be realized.

2. Consider items of significance: Not all incentives are created equal— at least not in the minds of workers. While one set of workers may find a financial incentive most attractive, others may be more enthusiastic about flexible work hours, more latitude in selecting job assignments, or greater likelihood of promotion.

   To some degree, the choice of incentives is a function of the constitution of the workforce. While millennials (workers born after 1980) are more likely to have interest in incentives that speak to community, individuality, and flexibility, their older counterparts (e.g., baby boomers, workers born between 1945 and 1960) are more likely to exhibit tendencies such as loyalty to the company, and may assign greater value to incentives that speak to job security and post-retirement financial security.

3. Validate incentives with workforce: This variability in interests and values within the workforce is why the leadership should solicit feedback from employees before committing to a particular incentive program. Although polling large workforces is difficult and often results in large numbers of conflicting and competing proposals, a small representative group (fewer than 10 or so people) can be gathered together and a facilitated discussion held, with the clearly established intent of settling on a single form of incentive.

4. Define the basis and extent of the incentives: The reason for settling first on the general form of the incentive is that the actual structure of the incentive program needs to be carefully designed and must factor in both the workers' interests and the company's goals and allowances for such programs. An open-ended program, one with no fixed limits, is harder to administer and control than a program with fixed components. For example, financial incentives might be tied to both schedule and workers' salaries, or additional vacation time might be aligned with cost reductions that the company can use to offset the hiring of temporaries to cover protracted vacation periods.

5. Communicate the program and protocols: Like all aspects of the transformation process, active communications need to be sustained with the workforce. In the case of incentives, this same expectation

applies. A communication strategy should be established that addresses the launch of the incentive program, the dissemination of details on how the program will work (e.g., extent/timing of incentives).

6. Implement the incentive program: Put in place the necessary infrastructure to administer the incentive program. This capability should include a basic tracking system that monitors the awards earned, metrics that can be distributed to all employees on a routine basis showing progress toward earning the incentives and—if the incentives are variable—the value of the potential incentive at any point in the transformation process. (This might be the case, for instance, if the program was designed so that earnings increased for each month ahead of schedule that the transformation team completes its work.)

7. Monitor awards/celebrate successes: In the case of awarding incentives, more is better; frequently is a goal. Sustained enthusiasm for an incentive program is amplified by word-of-mouth discussions among the workforce: The more they can personalize the results of the program, the more attention it gets; the more attention it gets, the more buy-in from employees (Rewards and Employee Benefits Association 2018).

Clarifying the Path Forward

The next step in putting the transformation project into action is to provide a straightforward and crisp description of the actual process. At this point in the transformation, the vision is clear, expectations have been established, and the incentive program put in place. So, what happens next? The more complete the explanation of the process, the easier to implement.

Given the magnitude of anticipated change, the transformation may be greeted by concern and skepticism. As with the incentives, the workforce has to be shown that the achievement is a matter of completing a series of well-defined steps—not a difficult and overwhelming revolution. As example, Figure 4.4 is a simple flowchart we developed for use at the

STREAMLINED TRANSFORMATION REVIEW PROCESS

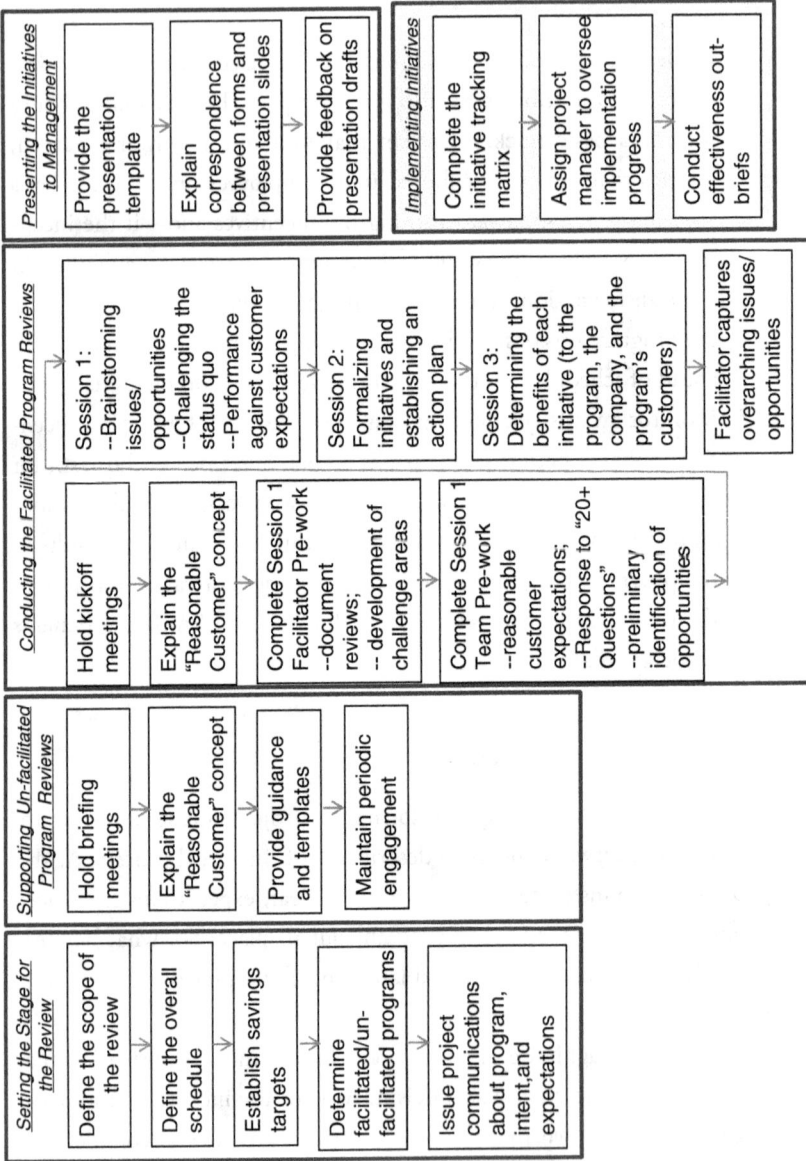

Setting the Stage for the Review

- Define the scope of the review
- Define the overall schedule
- Establish savings targets
- Determine facilitated/un-facilitated programs
- Issue project communications about program, intent, and expectations

Supporting Un-facilitated Program Reviews

- Hold briefing meetings
- Explain the "Reasonable Customer" concept
- Provide guidance and templates
- Maintain periodic engagement

Conducting the Facilitated Program Reviews

- Hold kickoff meetings
- Explain the "Reasonable Customer" concept
- Complete Session 1 Facilitator Pre-work
  - --document reviews;
  - --development of challenge areas
- Complete Session 1 Team Pre-work
  - --reasonable customer expectations;
  - --Response to "20+ Questions"
  - --preliminary identification of opportunities

- Session 1:
  - --Brainstorming issues/opportunities
  - --Challenging the status quo
  - --Performance against customer expectations
- Session 2: Formalizing initiatives and establishing an action plan
- Session 3: Determining the benefits of each initiative (to the program, the company, and the program's customers)
- Facilitator captures overarching issues/opportunities

Presenting the Initiatives to Management

- Provide the presentation template
- Explain correspondence between forms and presentation slides
- Provide feedback on presentation drafts

Implementing Initiatives

- Complete the initiative tracking matrix
- Assign project manager to oversee implementation progress
- Conduct effectiveness out-briefs

Figure 4.4 Framework for the transformation process

beginning of one transformation project. As the figure depicts, the process was designed to unfold in five major segments:

- Setting the stage for the review
- Supporting un-facilitated reviews (the functions that were minimally affected by the transformation—e.g., human resources—that were provided ongoing guidance but did not require dedicated attention from a transformation expert)
- Conducting the facilitated reviews: Teams assigned dedicated transformation support
- Presenting the initiatives to management—obtaining feedback and getting authorization to implement the transformation activities
- Implementing initiatives—monitoring, assessing, and re-enforcing progress in completing transformation tasks

As a first step, leadership selects team leads, individuals assigned responsibility for transforming a specific function, product, or service, individuals who will work with the transformation facilitators to complete the process. Team leads are selected based on certain attributes they have exhibited—a strong work ethic, a commitment to quality and safety, a willingness to challenge existing policies and protocols, and a positive reputation among co-workers.

Team leads are assigned the following responsibilities:

- Select four to six team members, representing individuals who are knowledgeable about the process or functions and including at least one internal customer (preferably someone who is known to have voiced issues with the quality or performance of the function)
- Set the schedule for meetings; complete any preparatory materials
- Establish the tone for the meetings (candid, honest, collaborative, challenging)
- Get input/feedback from other members of the organization as the team pushes forward with its efforts
- Provide status information to all other teams (progress, issues, interface expectations)

- Maintain the team's tight focus on the target (delivering on expectations)
- Develop and deliver the team's recommendations to the leadership

All of this groundwork needs to be underpinned by a robust communication strategy—one that details the process, the key messages, and the planned communication products. This strategy, reflective of the leadership's thinking, is intended to address and remain active throughout the entire transformation period—from launch to conclusion. Figure 4.5 is an example of a communication plan.

Working with the Teams

The basic process that we follow with the transformation teams involves four major steps:

- An introductory meeting with the team
- A meeting to develop a general picture of the function/product/or service
- A meeting to begin defining the improvement and transformation opportunities
- A meeting to evaluate and characterize the opportunities

Although targeted for 2 hours, each of the meetings is scheduled for 3 hours to allow for additional time when a team is actively—and sometimes heatedly—engaged in the discussion or is in the process of arriving at a breakthrough moment. When additional time is needed, each step can involve more than one meeting of the team. In addition, the meetings are scheduled for at least a week in between.

One thing we have found is that the time in between meetings allows team members to think individually and collectively about the conclusions reached, to talk with other workers, and to interact with other teams to gain additional perspective, insights, and evaluations of the team's efforts. Allowing for this period for rethinking team conclusions is of significant value (particularly between meetings 2 and 3), when goals are being solidified and are being characterized in readying for presentation to the leadership. Often, during these interim periods between meetings, team members may reassess their decisions—deciding, for instance, that some

Key Messages:
- We must undergo a transformation to ensure we are appropriately positioned to maintain and expand capabilities and sales in the near future.
- We are conducting a bottoms up, in-depth review that will include input from all employees. The idea is to engage as many employees possible to identify cost savings and process improvements.
- The majority of the cost savings that are identified will be used for important infrastructure improvements. This will ensure we are well positioned for future operations. We will share 50% of the fee earned on the cost savings with employees.
- This is a great time for out-of-the-box thinking and to ask the question: What can we do differently to improve processes and save money?
- We need all employees to fully participate in the exercise; the best ideas come from the people who are actually doing the work.

Proposed Communications Schedule:

Date	Action	Lead	Audience
---	Disseminate kick-off message	---	All employees
---	Provide talking points & template to managers to use in kicking-off non-facilitated meetings with management teams	---	Managers participating in non-facilitated meetings
---	Distribute "Why we're doing this" fact sheet	---	All managers / employees
---	Weekly update reminders via email and electronic signage	---	All employees
---	Status message	---	All employees
---	Wrap-up message	---	All employees

Communication Products:
- President kick-off message
- Fact sheet – Why we're doing this
- Weekly "Did You Know?" email & electronic signage messages/factoids
- President status message
- President wrap-up message

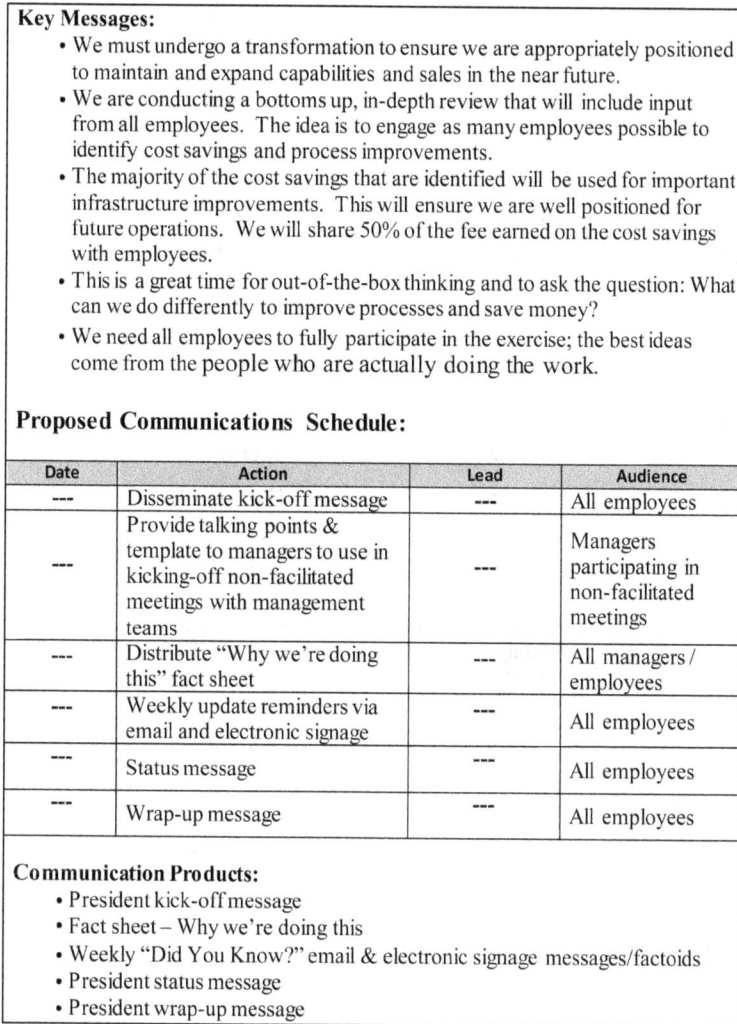

Figure 4.5 Sample communications plan

initial proposals are not feasible, recommendations may require further analysis, or that important considerations have been overlooked.

Introductory Meeting

In addition to having the team members get to know each other, the initial meeting is used to go over the reasons for the transformation, the company expectations, and the workings of the incentive program. It is also this first meeting that is important in engendering an expectation that the team will promote creativity, that it recognizes the importance of seeking the most appropriate means to achieve the transformation in their respective work functions.

One means of achieving this objective is by offering a set of challenge questions, questions that focus the team's attention on whether the prevailing requirements are relevant or applicable to the function as transformed, whether the source of the requirements is still of immediate concern in setting the new design, and what kinds of recommendations and criticisms the team members have heard that need to be factored into the team's deliberations.

A common series of questions we frequently employ, shown in Figure 4.6, is also intended to elicit the team's thinking about such matters

---

CHALLENGE QUESTIONS FOR ENCOURAGING CREATIVE THINKING ABOUT TRANSFORMATION

REQUIREMENTS:

1. What requirements are there for the program? Are these requirements established by regulation (including DOE Orders), by the company, or by the program?
2. Are there any requirements for which a waiver or other relief should be pursued?

INTERNAL CUSTOMERS:

3. What types of comments, complements, or complaints have you heard from customers?
4. Which of your products / processes do your internal customers value most / least?
5. Do you understand and are you meeting your customers' expectations?
6. Are there aspects of your job that customers need to better understand?

PROCESSES / PRODUCTS:

7. What processes or products could your program do better / differently?
8. Are there processes or products that you feel have little or limited value?
9. Are there processes you consider particularly onerous?
10. Are there process / products that entail routine rework?
11. If you were to redesign the entire program, what would you change (first, second)?
12. What program changes do you think would improve the morale of the group?
13. What would be the consequence of not delivering your products on time?

STAFFING:

14. Does the staff have the right expertise and experience to make the program successful?
15. Could changing people's work assignments reduce rework / interfaces / costs?
16. Are there functions assigned to subcontracts that could be assimilated by full-time staff ?
17. Is staffing based on routine operations or to accommodate inefficiencies?
18. Is training required that you feel is in excess of what you need to do your job effectively?
19. Do you feel everyone in the group is fully utilized?

GENERAL:

20. If you had one thing that you could ask senior management, what would that be?
21. Have you established and are you using metrics to monitor the program's performance?
22. What other tools do you use / need to ensure quality program performance?
− What other considerations should be evaluated in assisting in the transformation?

Figure 4.6 Sample questions for encouraging creative thinking

as the appropriateness of staffing levels and what procedures or protocols might be modified or eliminated.

The group is encouraged to take risks, define new boundaries, and challenge each other as regards their answers to the questions. In particular, this interaction is one reason why the teams tend to be most productive when at least one member has already demonstrated a willingness to cite areas where customers are not satisfied and to provide insights about any products or services that are considered of a lesser quality than they should be—in other words, helps to shape the perception of what constitutes a product that would satisfy the expectations of a reasonable customer. In this first meeting it might be said that safe is the enemy of progress; challenge is the path to opportunity.

At the conclusion of this first meeting, the schedule for the following meetings is set. Generally, setting meetings at the same time and place each week is the most accommodating for the team members' work schedules. Yet, irrespective of the logistics agreed upon by the team, it is essential to stress that an individual's absence from any meeting jeopardizes the team's—and ultimately, the company's—success. Accordingly, after completing the first round of introductory meetings with each of the teams, the overall schedule is posted in breakrooms and on the company's intranet (Figure 4.7).

Transformation Meeting Summary						
Program Team	Team Lead	Team Meetings				Presentation Developed
		Kickoff	Session 1	Session 2	Session 3	
Training						
Procedures						
Safety / IH						
Maintenance						
Engineering						
Fire Protection						
Work Control						
RadCon						
HR						
Procurement						
Environmental Protection						
Contractor / Quality Assurance						

Figure 4.7 Sample format for scheduling team meetings

Putting the Function in Perspective

Prior to the first meeting, the facilitator conducts an examination of relevant documentation. Generally looking at procedures, protocols, drawings, policies, and lesson learned reports will provide a range of questions that can be used to spark the work of the team. The goal of these questions is to get the conversation started more tangibly focused on the particular areas of transformation assigned to the team and to promote the concept that challenging the status quo is a primary means for achieving the transformation.

The session then works through one of two formats we have developed for putting the function or service in perspective. The two formats integrate elements of LEAN manufacturing practices with approaches and concepts we have developed, for example, examining the expectations of a reasonable customer. This meeting culminates in completing one of two transformation planning forms (either Figure 4.8 or Figure 4.9) depending on the types of information deemed most crucial by the team in completing the transformation and most suitable to capturing the essence of the team's discussion. A copy of a completed form is provided in Figure 4.10.

Transformation Planning
Essential Attributes to Be Considered

Function		
Phase 1: Confirming the Scope		
1. Customer Expectations	2. Current State	3.Delta
Phase 2: Transforming the Processes		
4. Processes Evaluated: Function not performing in excess of requirements /customer expectations ☐ Movement of information is timely / accurate / complete ☐ Rework has been eliminated ☐ Process is straightforward / no extraneous steps or motions ☐ Appropriate monitoring controls / metrics in place ☐ Personnel actively engaged in process design / improvement ☐	5, Matrix actions	
6. Actions Needed for Resolution of Phase 1 & 2 Reviews	7. Identify metrics/controls to ensure performance	8. Actions incorporated into Transition Plan

Figure 4.8 Transformation planning form—Option 1

Transformation Review Form (Step 1)

Program:	Prime Program Documents:	Team Members:		

Phase 1. Confirming the Scope

Primary Functions:	Primary Contractual / Regulatory Drivers / Requirements:	Internal Customers:	Internal Customer Expectations:	Consequences if process not effectively performed:

Phase 2. Assessing the Process:

Process Evaluation				Process Evaluation Comments and Considerations	
Evaluate Questions Using Perspective of Primary Internal Customers	Team Consensus			Issues:	Opportunities:
	Yes	No	Partially		
Function performing consistent with requirements and customer expectations (i.e., not overdesigned or overstaffed)					
Movement of information is timely / accurate / compete					
Rework has been eliminated					
Process is straightforward (No extraneous or unnecessarily complex actions)					
Appropriate monitoring controls / metrics in place					
Acceptable performance documented					
All affected personnel have had input to design / enhancements					
Other significant evaluative criteria					

Figure 4.9 Transformation planning form—Option 2

Transformation Planning
Essential Attributes to Be Considered

Function: Warehousing

Phase 1: Confirming the Scope

1. Customer Expectations	2. Current State	3. Delta
Store anything in any location Immediate availability of replacements, supplies	Projects try to plan ahead to order too much, limiting storage space Material is touched too many times Large volumes of abandoned supplies, equipment	Must maintain leases, but improve storage processes Educate management on consequences of over-ordering and abandoning equipment

Phase 2: Transforming the Processes

4. Processes Evaluated:	5. Matrix actions
Function not performing in excess of requirements /customer expectations ☐ Movement of information is timely / accurate / complete ☐ Rework has been eliminated ☒ Process is straightforward / no extraneous steps or motions ☐ Appropriate monitoring controls / metrics in place ☒ Personnel actively engaged in process design / improvement ☒	Excess material stored Engage property management in inventories Excess all unwarranted inventory Establish on-demand subcontracts

6. Actions Needed for Resolution	7. Identify metrics/controls to ensure performance	8. Actions incorporated into Transition Plan
Area closures initiated Inventory disposition implemented Coordination established with property management Management training underway On-demand subcontracts being solicited	New inventory metrics established—abandoned property, replenishment	Further on-demand subcontracts being identified

Figure 4.10 Example completed transformation planning form

Determining the Path for Transformation Implementation

Meetings 2 and 3 focus first on identifying the transformation activities and opportunities and then evaluating the benefits from each of those activities. Often the efforts during this session are representative of the types of activities and result in the types of products similar to those of LEAN manufacturing techniques, such as the production of a process flowchart assembled from wall-length sets of sticky notes detailing both current and future approaches to conducting business.

Each of the activities identified in these sessions is assigned an owner and an approximate completion date. So as to have a general sense of the schedule for delivering the activity, we start off with targeting completions within a general period of time, for instance setting initial targets as 45 days. The goal is to foster success, not to create challenges that may prove discouraging if not met.

Whatever the timeframes set for completing initiatives and actions, the framework should be consistent with the leadership's expectation and the award periods established in the incentive program. As we have emphasized, accomplishments that can be rewarded frequently are more apt to promote enthusiasm for the transformation project than ones that appear far out on a distant horizon.

As an interim step between Session 2 and Session 3, the team is asked to do some further thinking on how the recommendations and opportunities they are considering will play out. In so doing, as a team, they complete a summary analysis form (Figure 4.11) for use in Session 3.

INITIAL ANALYSIS					
Change:					
Transition Expectations	Issues	Context	Options	Recommendations	Implementation Steps

Figure 4.11 Form used to document the initial analysis

Session 3 picks up the discussion regarding proposed actions and opportunities. Amplifying the information developed in Session 2, the emphasis is on two considerations: (a) detailing precisely what types of benefits and what magnitude of benefit is likely to accrue, and (b) clarifying the types of benefits anticipated: Will the benefit be in cost savings, schedule acceleration, customer satisfaction, etc.? There is also effort at this time to determine if there are ancillary benefits, such as advancing the efforts of another transformation team. The team is encouraged to thoroughly assess the recommendations, discussing not only the benefits, but also the feasibility, the resources needed, and the barriers that may limit the probability of success.

The result of these efforts is the draft of the team's presentation to company leadership. Presentations to the leadership are planned at a general level of specificity (with minimal supporting technical detail) to allow for multiple team presentations to take place over a limited space of time. Completing all team presentations within no more than a 2-week period allows executives opportunity to assimilate ideas and increases likelihood of them recognizing correspondences or conflicts among the paths and recommendations being made by the teams.

Moreover, although presentations are prepared at a generalized level, company leaders are often inclined to delve deeply into the intricacies of any proposal, especially if that presentation requires significant costs or represents a major shift away from established company traditions and orthodoxy. (Figures 4.12 and 4.13 are the forms used to record the results from team meetings 2 and 3, respectively.)

As examples of a product from this phase of the transformation, Figure 4.14 provides a redesign of the flow of material within a complex waste processing facility. These types of graphic depictions are strongly encouraged in the development of the team recommendations; given the company leaders are listening to multiple presentations, retention of key points is increased through the use of images. The images also enhance other teams' understanding of the proposals.

Transformation Planning Form

Program:

Team Members:

Phase 3. Determining Actions Needed to Improve Process (resolve issues / take advantage of opportunities)

Near-Term Actions (<45 days)	Responsible Individual	Completion Date	
		Proposed	Actual
1			
2			
3			
Longer-Term Actions			
1			
2			
3			

Figure 4.12 Session 2 form

Transformation Planning – Session 3				
Program	Team Members			
Phase 4. Quantifying Improvements				
Efficiency / Timeliness	Savings		Customer Satisfaction	Indirect benefits / Related Opportunities
	Labor	Non-Labor		
Proposed Metrics to Ensure Sustained Performance				
Team Member Signatures				

Figure 4.13 Session 3 form

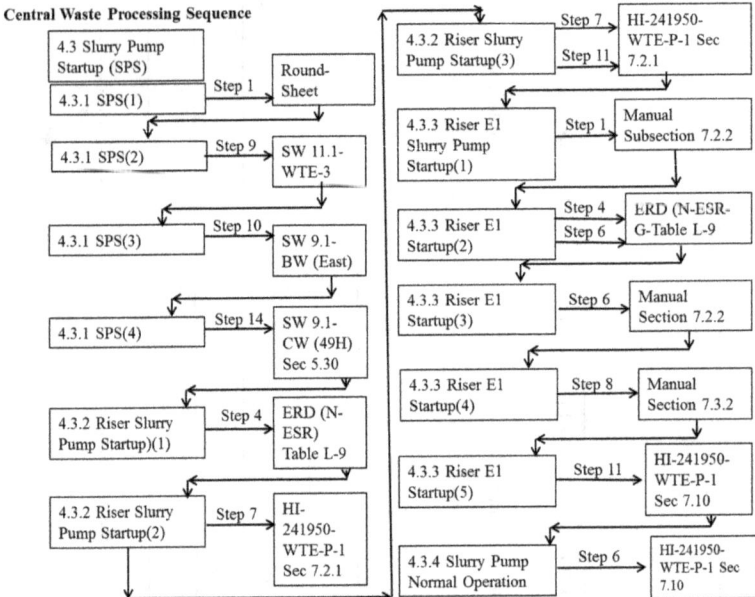

Figure 4.14 Transformation of a waste processing operation

Pulling It All Together—A Demonstrated Success Story

As a means of adding perspective and allowing a more encompassing picture of the entire process involved in working with transformation teams, Figures 4.15 through 4.21 depict the sequence of steps completed by a team assigned responsibility for rethinking the acquisition program that was one of the foundational components for transforming a multi-billion-dollar transportation corporation. Consistent with the expectations established by the company leadership, this team was successful in delivering a comprehensive response that represented the following attributes:

1. Overall process was made simpler so as to expedite procurements and minimize the time and number of instances the internal customers were required to engage in the process.

2. Distributed procurement capability was established. Appointed field personnel were trained and authorized to execute basic requisitions/credit-card purchases/and limited releases against blanket orders and master agreements. This change transferred the authority from the procurement staff to internal customers for completing basic and repetitive procurements—reducing the assistance needed from procurement personnel and reducing paperwork and administrative controls.

3. More effective reviews, with comments and feedback, were incorporated early in the requisition process, enhancing quality of requisition and eliminating rework, redundant and iterative review cycles, and delays in the processing of procurements.

4. A streamlined requisition pathway for procurement of critical components and safety was established, fast-tracking the acquisition of essential procurements.

5. Formal records documented reviews and comment resolution, enhancing documentation and augmenting the history needed for routine government audits. The improvement in documentation contributed to eliminating potential fines and expedited completion of required independent audits by regulatory agencies.

6. Clearly defined receipt actions (e.g., receipt inspection, property tagging) were built into the process; this coordination and early communication eliminated previously experienced problems with

suspect parts, improper storage, and delays in release of equipment to customers—all of which contributed to delays, waste, and customer dissatisfaction.

The pathway to delivering on the customer's expectations included production of a general plan and schedule, a structuring of assignments to maximize resource utilization, an evaluation of the staffing history, a re-evaluation of previous enhancement initiatives (including ones still underway), a brainstorming of issues and requirements, a revamped acquisition and change processes, and development of an innovative tool for tailoring requirements to subcontracts rather than requiring all technical subcontracts to respond to (and charge for) the same suite of requirements whether or not they were applicable to the work. (For instance, certain transportation regulations were only applicable for long hauls, but, yet, were assigned to all subcontracted hauling.)

To make the process clear, the next five figures lay out the development path followed by the team:

- Figure 4.15 represents the general game plan for the transformation of the procurement processes, calling out the primary elements that needed to be addressed by the team.
- Figure 4.16 establishes the questions the team set out to answer, partitioned into separate components of the planned transformation.

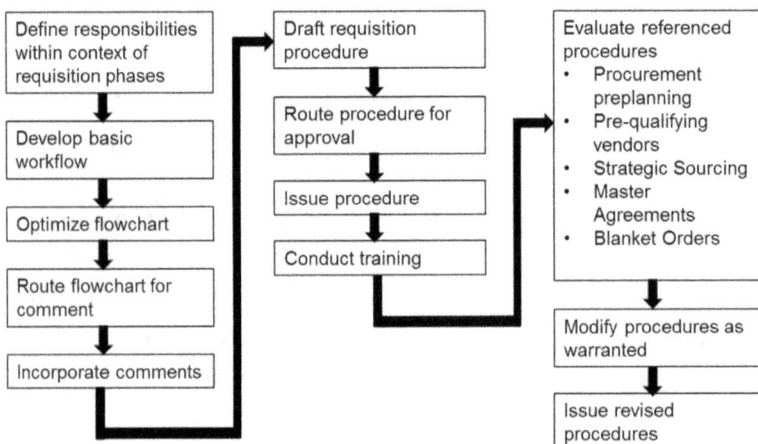

Figure 4.15 Generalized process for proceeding with transformation efforts

INITIATIVE 1: SIMPLIFIED REQUISITION FORM			
FACTORS	PROPOSED APPROACH	ISSUES TO RESOLVE	SEQUENCE
Training and Preparation			
Who can initiate a requisition?			
What procurement training is required (for whom and why)?			
What other documents / procedures are essential to the process?			
Preparing the Requisition			
What information does the requester need to provide?			
What quality levels are needed (why and when)?			
In what form is the information provided?			
Reviewing and Approving the Requisition			
Who has to review the requisition and for what specific purpose?			
is there a time limitation on reviews?			
Who approves the requisition?			
Processing the Requisition			
What steps does the buyer take to place / cancel the requisition?			
How is the request delivered to the vendor?			
Receipt of Materials			
What is done to ensure timely fulfillment / receipt of the order?			
What tracking is provided to the requester during the process?			
What confirmation ensures the order is correct?			
What is done if any component of the order is not correct?			
Documentation Retained			
What documentation of receipt is kept?			
What files documenting the requisition process are maintained?			
How is Accounts Payable notified an invoice for payment is due?			

Figure 4.16 Determining the type of information and detail required

- Figure 4.17 is the form used by the team to solicit input both from team members and from colleagues on other transformation teams.
- Figure 4.18 translates the efforts into assignment of and protocols for three subteams assigned to: (a) simplify the requisition process, (b) restructure the forms and procedures, and (c) develop new requisition practices designed to improve customer satisfaction and overall performance of the requisition process.

PROCUREMENT PLANNING COMMENT FORM			
DATE (IF MEETING HELD)	ITEM / SERVICE BEING PROCURED		
COMMENT / TOPIC OF DISCUSSION	PROPOSED DISPOSITION	IMPLEMENTATION (ACTION TO BE TAKEN)	
ATTENDEES / REVIEWERS			
ORG	SIGNATURE	ORG	SIGNATURE
REQUESTER		PROCUREMENT	
ENGINEERING		SAFETY	
QA		TRAINING	
Signing attests to agreement with disposition of issues and actions to be taken			

Figure 4.17 Sample comment form for soliciting perspectives and recommendations

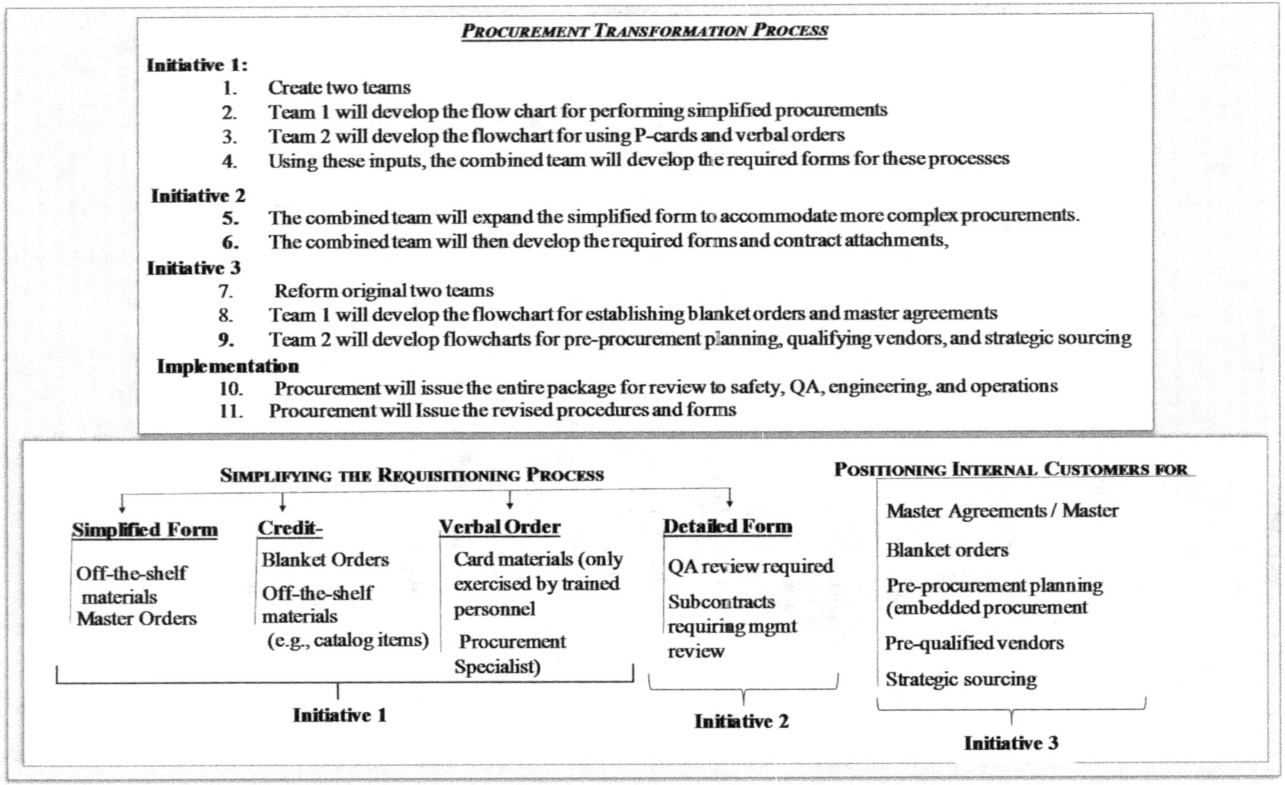
PROCUREMENT TRANSFORMATION PROCESS
Initiative 1:
1. Create two teams
2. Team 1 will develop the flow chart for performing simplified procurements
3. Team 2 will develop the flowchart for using P-cards and verbal orders
4. Using these inputs, the combined team will develop the required forms for these processes
Initiative 2
5. The combined team will expand the simplified form to accommodate more complex procurements.
6. The combined team will then develop the required forms and contract attachments,
Initiative 3
7. Reform original two teams
8. Team 1 will develop the flowchart for establishing blanket orders and master agreements
9. Team 2 will develop flowcharts for pre-procurement planning, qualifying vendors, and strategic sourcing
Implementation
10. Procurement will issue the entire package for review to safety, QA, engineering, and operations
11. Procurement will Issue the revised procedures and forms
SIMPLIFYING THE REQUISITIONING PROCESS
Simplified Form
Off-the-shelf materials
Master Orders
Credit-
Blanket Orders
Off-the-shelf materials
(e.g., catalog items)
Verbal Order
Card materials (only exercised by trained personnel
Procurement Specialist)
Detailed Form
QA review required
Subcontracts requiring mgmt review
Initiative 1
Initiative 2
POSITIONING INTERNAL CUSTOMERS FOR
Master Agreements / Master
Blanket orders
Pre-procurement planning (embedded procurement
Pre-qualified vendors
Strategic sourcing
Initiative 3

Figure 4.18 Establishing a structure for the sub-teams

- Figure 4.19 provides a matrix documenting details from research the team conducted relative to practices, staffing, previous and proposed initiatives, and the potential barriers to implementation.

With the planning and all three team sessions completed, the team then proceeded to turn the concepts into tangible solutions. Figures 4.20 and 4.21 present two of the final products that are, at once, representative of the magnitude of the transformation and also that suggest the success in addressing a range of long-standing issues that had, in part, engendered the transformation project.

The first product is a flowchart showing an abbreviated depiction of the revised acquisition process. The second product is one of a number of checklists that were developed that integrated the work of technical subject matter experts with the that of procurement staff in generating scope-specific lists of requirements that were subsequently incorporated into each subcontract. Using this tool, the process of drafting subcontracts was

FY-21 Procurement Staffing Projections						
	Current Status			**FY-21 Plan**		
Subfunction	**Current Staffing**		**Cost saving / staff reduction initiatives 2018 - 2020**	**Projected Staffing**		**Potential Barriers to Implementation**
	Full time	**Staff Aug**		**Full time**	**Part time**	
Prime Contract Management	2	0	Activities also include reporting to corporation and stakeholders	2	0	——
Subcontract Administration / Purchasing	14	3	Cross training of staff supported by staff reassignments	12	2	Expanded scope and types of audits; Timely transfer of field files to Procurement
Subcontract Engineer	1		already at minimum staffing; no further reductions planned	1	1	Timely completion of field activities and file transfers
Contract Closeout	0	3	Provide Contract Closeout experts to accelerate closings	0	2	Open Disputes/ Arbitration /Litigation support
Staff Aug. Resources Management	1	0	Integrated with small business administration and reporting	1	0	Significant increases in Staff Augmentation subcontracts contracts (currently 132)
Small Business	0	0	Combined with Staff Augmentation	0	0	Increased compliance / reporting requirements
Credit-Card purchases	0	0	Absorbed into work responsibilities covered by Subcontract Administration / Procurement	0	0	Increased compliance / reporting requirements
Admin Assistant	1	0	Functions absorbed	0	0	——
FY-20 Staffing	**19**	**8**		**16**	**5**	
FY-19 Staffing	**26**	**8**		**FY-21 Plan**		

Figure 4.19 Documenting the research and the plan

TRANSFORMATION TEAM PROPOSED ACQUISITION

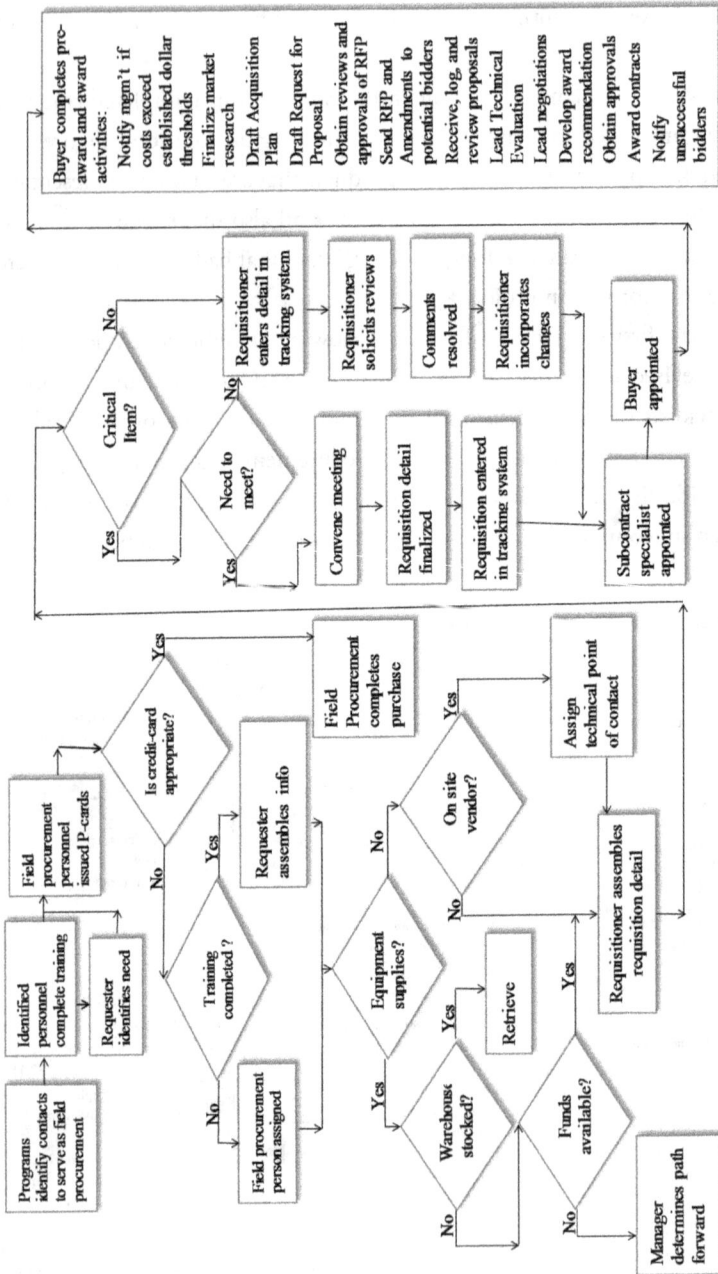

Buyer completes pre-award and award activities:

Notify mgmt if costs exceed established dollar thresholds

Finalize market research

Draft Acquisition Plan

Draft Request for Proposal

Obtain reviews and approvals of RFP

Send RFP and Amendments to potential bidders

Receive, log, and review proposals

Lead Technical Evaluation

Lead negotiations

Develop award recommendation

Obtain approvals

Award contracts

Notify unsuccessful bidders

Critical Item? — No → Requisitioner enters detail in tracking system → Requisitioner solicits reviews → Comments resolved → Requisitioner incorporates changes

Critical Item? — Yes

Need to meet? — No

Need to meet? — Yes → Convene meeting → Requisition detail finalized → Requisition entered in tracking system

Subcontract specialist appointed → Buyer appointed

Programs identify contacts to serve as field procurement → Identified personnel complete training → Requester identifies need → Field procurement personnel issued P-cards

Is credit-card appropriate? — Yes → Field Procurement completes purchase

Is credit-card appropriate? — No

Training completed? — Yes → Requester assembles info

Training completed? — No → Field procurement person assigned

Equipment supplies? — Yes

Equipment supplies? — No

On site vendor? — Yes → Assign technical point of contact

On site vendor? — No → Requisitioner assembles requisition detail

Warehouse stocked? — Yes → Retrieve

Warehouse stocked? — No

Funds available? — Yes

Funds available? — No → Manager determines path forward

Figure 4.20 Summary flowchart of transformed acquisition process

Exhibit G (Safety and Health) Applicability Matrix

Requisition/Contract Title:

Applicable	Revision No.	Contract Type	Construction Services	Tech Services	Staff Augmentation	Administrative	Items
		SH-4.1 - General Safety and Health Requirements					
	4.1.01	Safety Management Systems (ISMS)	M	M			
	4.1.02	Safety and Health Program	M	S			
	4.1.03	Hazard Communication	M	S			
	4.1.04	Explosives	S	S			
	4.1.05	First Aid and Emergency Response	M	S			
	4.1.06	Reporting Accidents and Incidents	M	S			
	4.1.07	Bulletin Boards	S	S			
	4.1.08	General Employee Training	M	M			
	4.1.09	Fire Protection - General	S	S			
	4.1.10	Emergency Preparedness/Management	S	S			
		SH-4.2 - General Safety and Health Requirements					
	4.2.01	General	M	S			
	4.2.02	Hazard Analysis	M	S			
	4.2.03	Inspections and Hazard Abatement	S	S			

M = Mandatory Requirement   S = Scope dependent requirement   Blank= To be completed by Subject Matter Expert

Figure 4.21 Example of a matrix developed to align requirements with subcontract scopes of work

redesigned, the precise requirements for the subcontract were made more immediately applicable to the work, the costs associated with subcontractors responding to unwarranted requirements were eliminated, and oversight of subcontractor work practice and performance was made more efficient and more effective.

Collectively, these and other products produced by the team addressed and satisfied all the expectations set by the leadership. The success in transforming this one function, in turn, contributed to the overall success of the company enterprise-wide transformation.

Getting Feedback from the Company Leadership

Having completed the sessions, the teams are now ready to bring their ideas forward to the leadership of the company. As we noted, given that the entire company is engaged in the transformation, a process is needed that is at once efficient and also standardized so as to allow the leadership to see correlations and anticipate conflicts among the proposals being proposed by the many teams. Were the teams simply allowed unilaterally to proceed with all their proposals, there may be issues with conflicting directions, competition for resources, concentration on changes of less significance than others, or activities that are out of sequence and therefore not as productive as would be desired.

To provide for a crisp and efficient set of presentations and discussions, teams are asked to follow a presentation format that highlights and summarizes information essential to allowing the leadership to make decisions and reach conclusions regarding whether initiatives are sufficiently thought through to warrant their authorization. In particular, the presentation focuses on high-level review of the following topics:

- List of primary functions
- Staffing history and projections
- Customer expectations (both internal and external)
- Significant changes and enhancements to the program over the period immediately (one year) prior to initiation of the transformation project (so as to make certain there are not major activities currently in transition that may affect the path forward)

- The proposed initiatives and the principal implementation steps
- The anticipated benefits from implementation
- The metrics or other monitoring techniques that will be employed

Figure 4.22 provides the format we employ for making presentations to the company leadership. As needed, multiple pages are used for any section needing more than a single slide; however, we generally work with the teams so as to ensure that the presentation—including allowance for questions and answers—can be completed in no more than 1½ to 2 hours.

Based on responses and authorizations provided by the leadership at the conclusion of each presentation, the initiatives are divided into three categories:

Category 1: Initiatives that have significant, broad impact/benefits and are authorized to proceed immediately with implementation

Category 2: Initiatives to be pursued once the category 1 initiatives are complete

Category 3: Initiatives that either are to be deferred for potential future implementation or need to be modified and re-presented

The decisions resulting from the presentations are recorded on a tracking sheet that tracks the following: the initiative goals and deliverables,

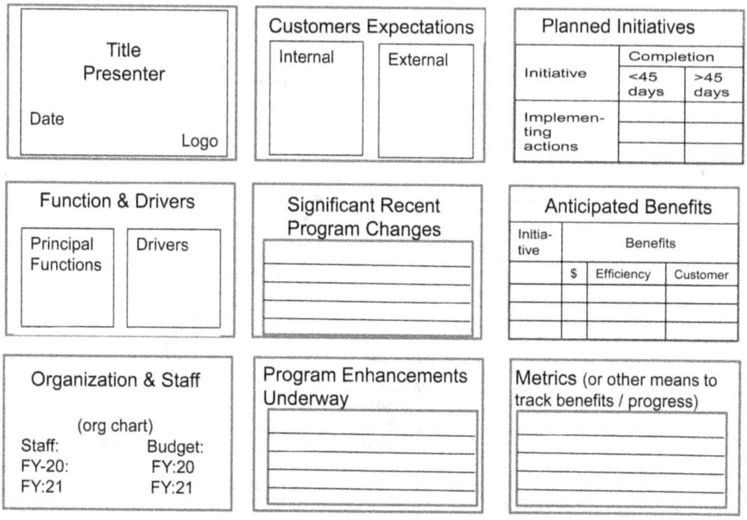

Figure 4.22 Slide format for use in leadership presentations

the principal actions required to achieve full implementation, notes and comments, and schedules (including the planned date for an effectiveness briefing—a meeting held with the leadership team generally 3 to 6 months after completing implementation to assess whether the projected benefits have been realized or—if not—what additional actions are warranted). (Figure 4.23 is a copy of the format for tracking implementation of initiatives. Figure 4.24 is a form showing several category 1 entries.)

Transformation Initiative Tracking Form				Implementation		Effectiveness Out-brief
Initiative	Goal / Deliverable	Lead	Participants	Principal Actions	Due Date	
Category 1 Initiatives (initiatives that have significant, broad impact)						
1						
2						
3						
Category 2 Initiatives (initiatives that will contribute substantively to operational performance, efficiency, and cost effectiveness)						
1						
2						

Figure 4.23 Initiative tracking form

Transformation Initiative Tracking Form			Implementation	
Initiative	Goal / Deliverable	Participants	Principal Actions	Effectiveness Out-brief
Category 1 Initiatives (initiatives that have significant, broad impact)				
1	Re-evaluate Engineered Design Levels (EDLs)		Work Control		TBD
2	Overhaul the Requisition Process	Provide a graded approach for acquisition and subcontracting processes	Quality Assurance Engineering	Revise programs and procedures	TBD
3	Streamline the Engineering Change Notice (ECN) process	Provide a graded approach to requirements for ECNs	Maintenance Work Control	Reduce signoffs	TBD
4	Redefine Un-reviewed Safety Question categorical exclusions	Limit USQ reviews to work packages with significant safety implications	Quality Assurance	Request authorizing agency approval	TBD
5	Revise QA plan to ensure appropriate engagement of QA in business / technical processes	Ensure QA involvement in required and audits	Engineering Procurement Maintenance		TBD
6	Determine scopes of work to be handled using skill of the craft	Establish scopes of work and controls for use of skill of the craft	Work Control Operations Maintenance	Identify suitable skill of the craft work scope	TBD

Figure 4.24 Example of Category 1 entries

As can be seen in Figure 4.24, the leadership team in this example authorized immediate implementation of initiatives across a range of functional areas: that is, requisitioning, quality assurance, engineering, information technology, and operations. As an illustration of the process by which one of these category 1 initiatives (Engineering Change Notices) evolved, Figure 4.25 shows related sections from parts of the team's presentation to the leadership.

Lastly, as has been mentioned, there is a need to keep enthusiasm up throughout the full duration of the transformation review. Having a coherent transformation process and attractive incentives must be complemented by a robust and continuous communication strategy. Just as

Transformation Focus: Engineering		Complete in 45 Days		Anticipated Completion Date
Transformation Opportunities and Initiatives		Yes	No	
Initiative	*Overhaul the Engineering Change Notice (ECN) process*			
Implementing Actions	a) Revise the ECN procedure and reduce signoffs and technical screening		X	60 – 90 days
	b) Develop a simplified ECN for balance of plant safety systems		X	60-90 days
	c) Eliminate requirement for a formal engineering evaluation and ECN for office buildings		X	45 – 60 days

Anticipated Benefits from Implementation						
Transformation Focus: Engineering						
	Benefits					
Initiative	*Hard dollar Savings*		*Improved Efficiency of Operations*	*Enhanced Customer Satisfaction*	*Schedule Acceleration*	*Other Benefits*
	Labor $	*Non-labor $*				
Overhaul the Engineering Change Notice (ECN) process	$100K year 1; $300k year 2 and 3	0	Reduces competition for engineering resources	Provides graded approach for approving projects Improves operations in construction, safety, and work control	Expedited reviews will reduce average schedules by 2 -3 months	Greater professional satisfaction: engineers not required to expend time on ancillary activities

Figure 4.25 Presenting Category 1 initiatives

Communication / Implementation Plan for Transformation Review

A)   Communication Strategy
1)   Explain what the transformation review was about, what was expected from each program, and the expected benefit (Quotation from CEO)
2)   Summarize Category 1 initiatives
3)   Establish on line posting of the complete set of initiatives
4)   Post status tracking forms in conference rooms
5)   Provide periodic updates on the progress / impact of initiatives
6)   Provide news stories about significant successes

B)   Implementation Strategy
1)   Compile a list of the initiatives
2)   Establish a "Project Manager" to monitor and track progress of initiatives
3)   Develop a methodology for quantifying actual savings and benefits
4)   Meet with program owners to review tracking form and solicit updates
5)   Establish a formal process / frequency for routine report updates
6)   Conduct "effectiveness out-briefs" 60 – 90 days after initiative complete

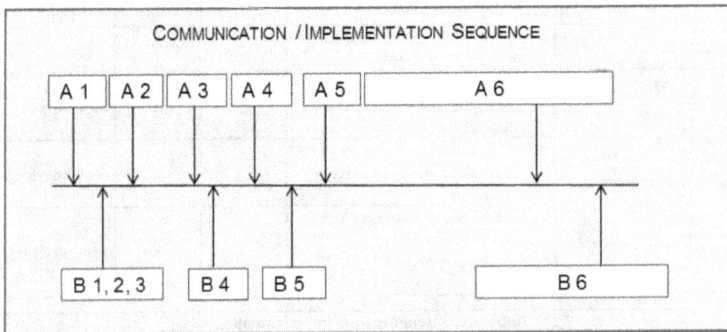

Figure 4.26 Example of an implementation period communication plan

a plan was needed to announce and sustain buy-in for the incentive program, so a communication program is needed once all the presentations have been completed and the lengthy process of implementation takes over. To this end, Figure 4.26 is an example of a postpresentation communication plan.

Conclusion

Ultimately, the success of the transformation project is contingent on the sustained support of the workforce. While the leadership creates a clear set of expectations and objectives and institutes a project management infrastructure sufficiently robust to monitor performance and progress, making the objectives a reality falls most particularly to the workforce.

The process and the tools used with the workforce to progress from expectation to tangible solutions and then to define and implement the requisite actions rely on a development process that is straightforward, easy to administer, and in keeping with the principles and concepts (e.g., reasonable customer) we have been advocating.

In the end, the success of the transformation venture rises or falls on maintaining an unflagging attention to the quality, timeliness, and completeness of communications between the leadership and the workers, within the individual work teams, and among the work teams. It relies on the commitment to endorsing creativity, innovation, and a trust in the capabilities of the workforce and in the transformation teams. It relies on fully utilizing the talent and experience base available within and across the company.

The tools and techniques shared in this chapter represent the solid bedrock needed to allow the efforts of the transformation project to flourish. Jointly, the company leadership and the company's workforce must share a common vision, a vision that recognizes that, in an adaptation of Lincoln's admonishment, "the best way to predict [the company's] future is to create it."

CHAPTER 5

The Final Set of Transformation Mechanics— Oversight

The Directors to have power to make all Bye-laws, rules and regulations requisite for conducting the affairs of the Company.

—Alexander Hamilton

Prospectus of the Society for Establishing Useful Manufactures, 1791

On February 2, 2014, the Seattle Seahawks beat the Denver Broncos in Super Bowl XLVIII by a score of 43 to 8. The score represented the largest margin of victory for an underdog, tied for the third largest point differential in Super Bowl history, and it was the first time the winning team scored in excess of 40 points. As astonishing as was the upset, another memorable event occurred during that game. At a cost of $4 million for its 30-second slot, RadioShack broadcast a commercial designed to display a reinvigorated corporation.

Two stunned RadioShack employees get a phone call telling them that "the 80s wants their store back." Immediately, an array of well-known characters emerges. Led by the wrestler Hulk Hogan; the gold-medal gymnast, Mary Lou Retton; a variety of animated and animatronic characters; and Alf, the central figure in a TV sit-com about a friendly extraterrestrial who crash-lands in the garage of a suburban middle-class family, the hoard ransacks the store. Then, consistent with the commercial's theme of corporate rejuvenation, the group loads the store's merchandise on top of an awaiting DeLorean—the 1980s' stainless-steel, gull-winged sports car that served as the time machine in the movie *Back to the Future*. As the DeLorean ostensibly speeds off to the future, the 80-year-old hardware-store image common to several thousand RadioShack stores is instantaneously replaced by the new RadioShack, a modern (almost futuristic) electronics emporium. The commercial closes by invoking RadioShack's new slogan "Let's Do It Together," a program wherein employees were going to be made available to assist customers with their electronics projects.

Unfortunately, despite the optimistic presentation of a new image and new concept for the company, the following year RadioShack entered bankruptcy, and shortly thereafter ceased to exist.

RadioShack had once been considered *the* place to go to purchase electronics, from basic components to one of the earliest home computers. Founded in Boston in 1921 by two London-born brothers, Theodore and Milton Deutschmann, the company—named after the compartment where wireless equipment was kept on boats—began by selling supplies to radio officers on ships. During a period of significant growth, the business opened retail stores in the Northeast, complemented by a mail-order electronics business.

After being bought out by Tandy Leather Company in 1963 for approximately $300,000, the company model concentrated on selling small items that could be heavily marked up, for example, accessories, batteries, transistors, and capacitors. The oil crisis of the early 1970s, the resulting imposition of a 55-mph speed limit, and a series of movies about free-wheeling truckers (e.g., *Smokey and the Bandit*) set off a craze in CB (Citizen Band) radios, boosting corporate sales. This success was followed by RadioShack's introduction of the first mass-produced personal computer—the TR-80, which offered roughly 16K of memory, a 12-in square monitor, one shade of gray characters, and no graphics. The company at this point was faring very well: In 1966 there were 100 stores nationwide; by 1971 there were 1,000, and at one point there would be more than seven times that number.

However, the string of successes was about to end. At the same time that the hardware business was shrinking, the TR-80 was overtaken by more aggressive companies entering the home computer market. Deciding to abandon the computer business in 1993, the company turned to its next principal venture: cell phones. However, this redirection had two significant flaws: (1) Signing up cell phone customers—as compared to handling small, over-the-counter sales—was a time-consuming process that shifted attention away from what had always been the company's customer base. (2) As the cell phone industry matured, it basically undermined much of RadioShack's market: Cell phones' expanding capabilities eliminated the buyers' market for many of the RadioShack's most profitable product lines such as voice recorders, GPS devices, answering machines, and camcorders (Dada 2016).

In its 2013 federal filing, the company laid out its cascading cavalcade of challenges. As was noted, RadioShack's "return to profitability" was contingent on a number of factors:

- Our ability to offer and sell products with sufficient gross profit to improve our overall profitability
- Our ability to benefit from capital improvements made to our stores
- Our success in attracting customers into our retail locations
- Our ability to choose the correct mix of products to sell
- Our ability to keep our retail locations stocked with merchandise customers will purchase
- Our ability to maintain fully staffed retail locations with appropriately trained employees
- Our ability to remain relevant to the customer.
  (U.S. Securities and Exchange Commission 2014)

As the company tried to shift back to profitability, it had already been outpaced by companies like Best Buy, Walmart, and Amazon that had established themselves in the world of Internet-based sales. Despite several attempts to revitalize its image, its services, and its inventory, RadioShack had fallen too far behind the competition to recover. In February 2015, RadioShack revealed it was preparing to close its doors for good: It had entered a bankruptcy arrangement in which Sprint would take over half of the stores and the remainder would be shuttered. The downward spiral had been hastened by a number of factors: RadioShack had not shown a profit in the previous 4 years, was in the process of being delisted from the New York Stock Exchange, had cycled through six CEOs in the period from 2004 to 2014, and was being sued by at least two different sets of disgruntled employees.

In a 2015 article entitled "A Eulogy for RadioShack," an ex-employee recounted the final days of the company—citing long days with few customers, outmoded inventory, overworked staff, and an adversarial relationship between workers and corporate management. In a single statement, the ex-employee effectively articulated the reason underpinning RadioShack's demise:

> This is a ... business ... built to work perfectly in the year 1975. The Internet comes around, and [we are] expected to move on it aggressively ... except basically *nobody* really understood the Internet ... So they whiffed big a few times. Then the iPhone came around and rendered half the stuff RadioShack sold completely redundant. This company needed to become something radically different ... I just don't think it knows how to be anything else. (Bois 2015)

Although there is a lot that went wrong in the undoing of the 80-year-old electronics giant, one factor that significantly contributed was the lack of effectiveness on the part of the company's board of directors. As the *Dallas Morning News* reported regarding one of the lawsuits filed against RadioShack, "with the complicity of RadioShack's conflicted CEO and faithless board of directors, delayed actions that could have preserved significant value in the company" cost the plaintiffs about $500 million (Wolf 2015). The board had essentially abdicated its responsibility when it came to shaping the company's strategic decision making, had been ineffective in selecting and overseeing the company's CEO, had minimally fulfilled its fiduciary obligations, and had failed adequately to represent the interests of the company, its employees, and its stakeholders (Silverman 2016).

Transformation and the Board of Directors

RadioShack's corporation bylaws offered a simple articulation of the expected role of its corporate board of directors: Article III, Section 1: "The business and property of the corporation shall be conducted and managed by a Board of Directors consisting of not less than three (3) members" (Law Insider 2011). This model of a board of directors descends from long-standing English roots. As early as 1694, the charter for the Bank of England (which initiated use of the term "directors") provided for a board of 24 directors to provide governance of its institution. When businesses began to flourish in America, this model was retained. In America, the concept of power over corporate management residing with an elected board dates back at least to an 1811 New York statute, generally acknowledged as the first general incorporation statute:

> the stock, property and concerns of such companys [*sic*] shall be managed and conducted by trustees, who, except for the first year, shall be elected at such time and place as shall be directed by the by laws of said company. (Gevurtz 2004)

Whether identified as Boards of Directors, Trustees, or Boards of Managers, the group chartered to assist in directing and maintaining the health of the company is intended to be independent of the company management and sufficiently knowledgeable and informed to assist in acting in the interest of the company—which includes being prepared to challenge and take positions in opposition to management when appropriate. This obligation is as true for a company undergoing a transformation as it is for a large company in a stable market environment.

Understanding the obligations of a board of directors can be summarized in terms of four ethical principles that have been recognized in the courts:

- Duty of care
- Duty of obedience
- Duty of loyalty
- Duty of candor

Duty of Care: Decisions must be made with due deliberation. The duty of care describes the level of competence expected of a Board member commonly expressed (similar to our reasonable customer concept) as the attention and effort an ordinary prudent person would exercise in a like position and under similar circumstances. In particular, decisions affecting the interests of the company should be based on informed, judicious judgment.

Duty of Obedience: The duty of obedience requires Board members to be faithful to the organization's mission and the rules/laws of the federal and state governments. They are not permitted to act in a way that is inconsistent with the central goals of the organization.

Duty of Loyalty: Directors must act "in the interest of the corporation" (and, implicitly, in the interest of its shareholders). As such, the duty of loyalty is a standard of faithfulness; a Board member must give undivided allegiance when making decisions affecting the organization. This means that a Board member can never use information obtained from his position for personal gain, but must act in the best interests of the organization.

Duty of Candor: As interpreted by the courts, this duty means that Board members have an obligation to disclose to shareholders all information that may be relevant to their evaluation of the company (Larcker and Tayan n.d.).

Assuming the board members have exercised the diligence expected of these four duties, the courts, under what is known as "the business judgment rule," will not second-guess the board's actions. This standard, in fact, was what contributed to RadioShack's success in the employee lawsuits filed against it; the courts found that the board had followed a reasonable process, had taken account of the relevant facts, and had made their decisions and had taken actions in "good faith"—even though the actions proved to be financially inappropriate (Moore 2014).

Given these four "duties," a board of directors is chartered to conduct a variety of activities in securing the performance and integrity of the company, including:

- Ensuring the continuity and sustainability of the company
- Approving corporate strategy
- Validating business models
- Identifying and monitoring key performance measures
- Directly overseeing the risk management program
- Selecting key executives

- Ensuring compliance with laws and regulations
- Ensuring the accuracy, thoroughness, and integrity of financial statements
- Approving major investments and purchases
- Protecting the company assets and reputation
- Representing the interest of shareholders (Bainbridge 2002)

Yet, as these factors make evident, in the case of RadioShack, good faith did not equal good judgment.

Given these considerations, it becomes clear how the board of directors relates to the transformation efforts of the company leadership and the company workforce. As shown in Figure 5.1, the leadership is accountable to establish the vision, translate the vision into a workable plan, and monitor the ongoing efforts to deliver on the expectations. The workforce, in turn, defines the mechanics of the transformation and provides the expertise that delivers the results. Overlooking the transformation, the board provides two major services: It validates

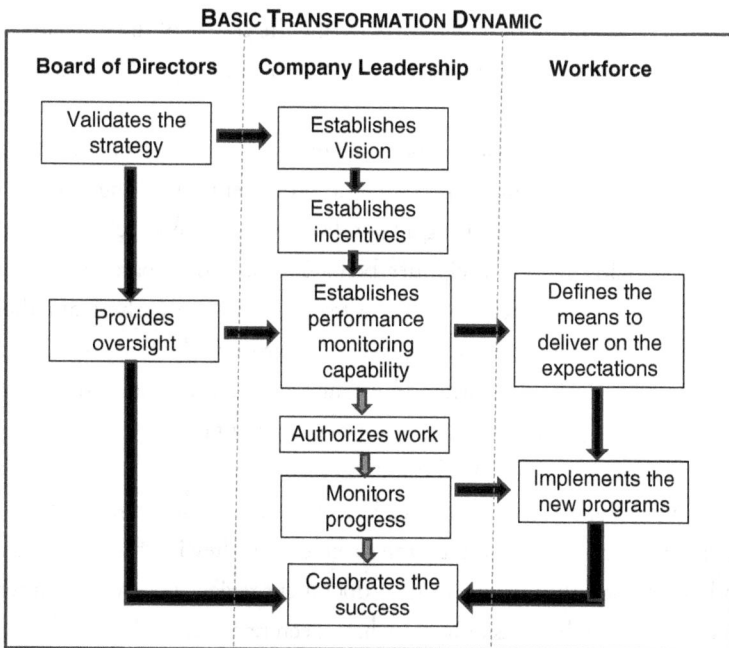

Figure 5.1 Interrelationship among the board of directors, company leadership, and the workforce

that the vision is realistic, achievable, and in the best corporate interests; and the board periodically monitors progress to ensure the transformation continues to represent the best interests of the company (Sonnenfeld 2002).

There are multiple means of fulfilling these responsibilities. If there is no board, as may be the case in small, privately owned businesses, then the activities may fall to the internal corporate leadership. In companies that have Boards consisting of full-time company managers and appointed board members, much of the work can be conducted by the board through standard committee structures (e.g., risk management, governance, finance); these committees, as their names imply, focus on the fundamentals of the business. However, by far the most common approach for fulfilling the oversight responsibility is a combination of activities conducted by the board and complemented by assessments undertaken by independent reviewers as contracted by the board.

As regards assessments, the two most important factors are (1) that the reviews have a degree of independence, and (2) assessments are undertaken at appropriate junctures during the course of the transformation (points critical to demonstrate and sustain the assigned course of the transformation).

As a starting point for independent reviews, the board or the Project Director determines the scope that warrants attention. Using corporate resources if they exist, or hiring a team from one of many technical agencies specializing in the disciplines being assessed, the board selects the team lead, who, in turn, selects the team. Collectively, the team then develops a schedule, makes assignments regarding which aspects of the scope each team member will address, and begins the review—most frequently starting with an examination of documentation (e.g., schedules, policies, procedures, technical drawings).

Having done this preliminary assessment, the team members draft their particular lines of inquiry, the specific areas they intend to examine, and the method they will be using—document review, observation, interviews. Once, all the lines of inquiry have been reviewed and the team lead is satisfied they are thorough and complimentary rather than conflicting or overlapping, the actual review is conducted.

Typically, daily briefings are held by the team with the Board or senior management to report out on any significant findings or problems. Then when all the team members have finished their individual reviews, a report is compiled. In advance of issuing a report, the team typically holds an out-brief with the board and management to present their results. Team conclusions are characterized in terms of four headings: (1) findings (issues requiring attention and correction), (2) recommendations (actions that would, in the opinion of the team, enhance cost, schedule, or technical performance, but, implementation of which are left to the discretion of the leadership), (3) areas of opportunity (aspects of the work that may warrant further investigation to determine if additional refinements are needed), and (4) best practices (recognition of activities and processes that are particularly noteworthy).

Subsequently, if requested by the board or project manager, the independent review team provides a formal written report. Depending on the nature of the reported results, the management may develop a formal corrective action plan to document and track the resolution of findings and, potentially, to track team-identified areas of opportunity. Figure 5.2 depicts the independent review process.

Although the types of reviews and the timing are determined by such factors as the scope of the transformation, the duration, the complexity, and the potential risks and challenges, assessments or independent reviews should be conducted at stages when the strategy and expectations have been set, when work is ready to be authorized, periodically during the implementation of the transformation activities, and then when the company is preparing to transition into the new enterprise.

Assessment of Strategy

The earliest review should take place when the leadership has determined the scope, purpose, and expectations for the transformation. The review is primarily designed to look at what is planned and the associated rationale. Table 5.1 provides a summary-level checklist for use in this initial review.

Assessment of Project Mechanics: Following agreement that the project's objectives and rationale are reasonable and supported by the Board's review, the next assessment should concentrate on determining if the

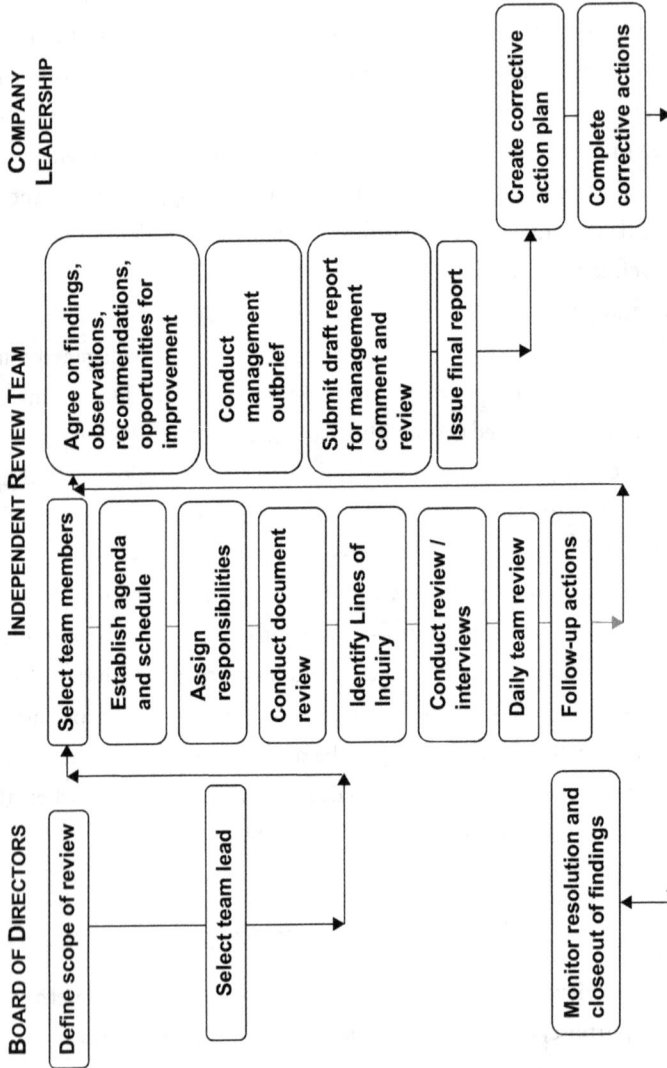

BOARD OF DIRECTORS

INDEPENDENT REVIEW TEAM

COMPANY LEADERSHIP

Define scope of review

Select team lead

Select team members

Establish agenda and schedule

Assign responsibilities

Conduct document review

Identify Lines of Inquiry

Conduct review / interviews

Daily team review

Follow-up actions

Agree on findings, observations, recommendations, opportunities for improvement

Conduct management outbrief

Submit draft report for management comment and review

Issue final report

Create corrective action plan

Complete corrective actions

Monitor resolution and closeout of findings

Figure 5.2 The independent review process

Table 5.1 Basics of the strategic assessment

General Purposes	Specific Areas of Interest
Validate that the project is feasible and the ratio-nale is credible	• Clear business justification commensurate with required investment • Appropriateness of proposed undertaking • Clear statement of the business problem • Validity of the business imperative • Understanding of the scope, primary risks, costs, and schedules • Framework for monitoring progress and identifying imple-mentation issues • Appropriate engagement of stakeholders, regulators, or others central to success • Confirmation that the project makes strategic sense (e.g., correctly anticipates market trends, customer base, tech-nology advances)

physical means of delivering on the expectations is also reasonable and achievable. Table 5.2 provides a checklist for use in conducting this assessment.

Performance Reviews: Once work has been authorized and transfor-mation activities are underway, periodic reviews should be conducted to

Table 5.2 Basics of the project management assessment

General Purposes	Specific Areas of Interest
Confirm technical logic, capability, and resource of the project Confirmation the or-ganization is ready and prepared to undertake the project	• Precision of goals and expectations, including common understanding of goals among leadership, workforce, and stakeholders • Sophistication of the performance management system (validation of Earned Value Management System for larger projects) • Review of schedules, WBS structure, project organization • Compliance with technical, regulatory, and industry requirements • Readiness of key technical components, e.g., design, engi-neering, quality assurance, construction • Extent of assets versus need for redesign—systems, data, business rules, procedures, and program delivery infrastructures • Controls for data migration; implementation of business/IT systems • Evaluation of the robustness of the risk management pro-gram and completeness of risk identification • General project management, including roles and responsibilities

ensure the project remains on course—cost, schedule, risks. Table 5.3 summarizes the subjects of interest that should be monitored during the implementation period.

Table 5.3 Basics of the performance assessments

General Purposes	Specific Areas of Interest
Validate that progress is consistent with the established schedule and cost	• Refinement of estimates and assumptions • Refinement of schedules • Currency of the identified risks • Review of safety records • Review of progress reports, quality assurance audits, and schedules • Review status of individual services and functions

Transition Assessment

When the work of transition is complete, a final assessment should be held to validate that the organization is ready for business as the new company. Table 5.4 provides the basics of this final pre-deployment assessment.

Table 5.4 Final transformation assessment

General Purposes	Specific Areas of Interest
To ensure the project is ready to proceed with the transformation	• Confirmation on a function-by-function and project basis that expectations have been met and projected outcomes will be achieved • All work activities are complete including required documentation, permits, etc. • Business systems are fully operational and project acceptance testing complete • Data, as appropriate, have been successfully migrated • Training is complete and documented • All risks have been closed out • The project is ready for transformation

Pulling together the scope and responsibility for the assessments, Figure 5.3 provides a summary of the stages at which assessments should be considered, the primary focus of each of the reviews, and the agent responsible (either the board of directors or an independent review team under the direction of the board.)

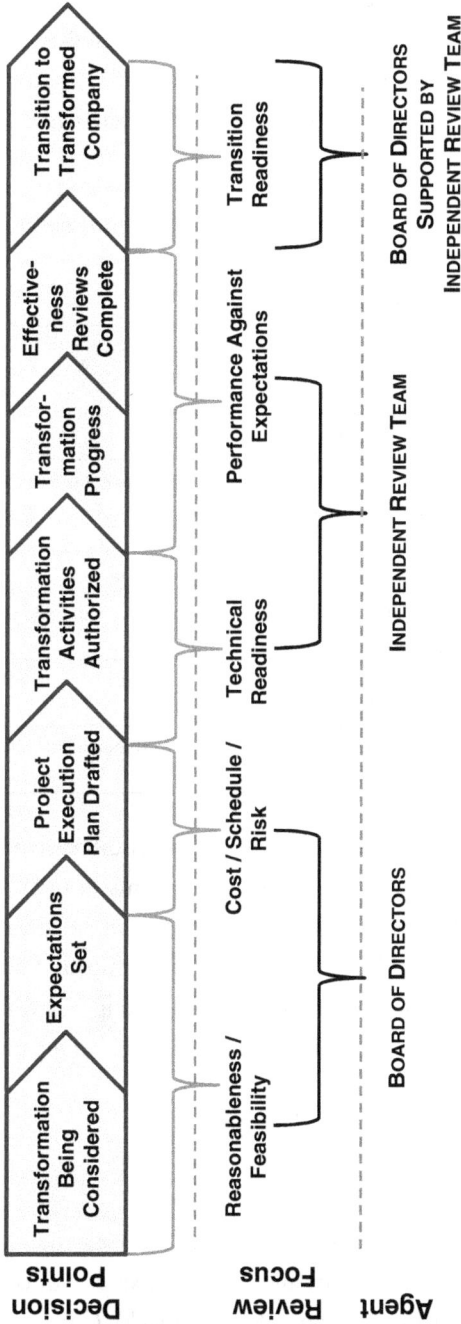

Figure 5.3 Sequencing of transformation project oversight activities

135

Although similar to the assessment structure just discussed, a slight variation may be necessary if the transformation involves significant amounts of design, engineering, and construction activity (e.g., building a new production facility). In those instances, the appropriate reviews from those listed in Table 5.5 should be integrated into the oversight program.

Table 5.5 Additional assessments when significant construction/ fabrication is involved

Review	Purpose
System requirements review	Ensure that system requirements have been thoroughly identified, reviewed, and understood
Preliminary design review	Ensure design is sufficiently complete to allow confirmation that systems will operate successfully
Critical design review	Demonstrate that detailed designs are complete, meet requirements, and are ready for fabrication and assembly
System qualification review	Ensure testing criteria are complete and will effectively demonstrate system capability and performance
System readiness review	Validate that system is ready for deployment and the design is ready for production
Operational test readiness review	Ensure system is ready for testing, with high confidence of its success
Operational readiness review	Validate system is ready for full commercial operation

In essence, the cumulative purposes of the assessments are to allow an independent verification of the essential elements of the transformation (Table 5.6). These independent reviews are not intended to set direction or usurp the responsibility or authority of the company leadership. They are intended to promote high confidence—among board members and stakeholders—that investments being made in the company's future are reasonable and prudent.

Conclusion

Returning for a moment to RadioShack, we can get a good summation of the role of a board of directors and its relationship with company management from Len Roberts, one of RadioShack's Chief Executive Officers. In an interview some years after leaving RadioShack, he made some

Table 5.6 Transformation oversight: The 10 essential questions

Success Criteria	All Tasks/Activities Complete		Expectations Achieved		Resolution Actions Required
	Yes	No	Yes	No	
1. Is performance being effectively monitored and appropriate adjustments made in a timely manner?					
2. Are all functions performing per expectations?					
3. Are all functions fully compliant with requirements/regulations/laws?					
4. Are safety and quality being maintained?					
5. Is all training complete, up-to-date, and documented?					
6. Have business systems and data been migrated, tested, and accepted?					
7. Have accurate and complete schedules been maintained?					
8. Have cost estimates been updated and maintained current?					
9. Have all significant risks been accounted for/monitored/and appropriately dispositioned?					
10. Will the transformation project when completed achieve all the established goals and expectations?					

salient points about the roles, responsibilities, and authorities of Boards of Directors. As he had perceived, "Board members are more important today than ever before; [they] are responsible for some key areas of the enterprise, especially in terms of holding management accountable for results and for the execution of strategy."

A key factor in positioning the board to hold management account-able was a reciprocal approach in which the board was kept informed and maintained in a decision-making role. As he advised in that article, individuals inclined to join companies as board members should do some advance checking:

> Make sure that it is a company that truly believes in the role of a highly engaged board, because there's nothing more boring to me than sitting around a table being 'presented to,' without the management team trying to leverage the valuable expertise around a board table.

Yet, as we have been discussing, at the same time all Board members should be appropriately circumspect about the roles they play. In a some-what sarcastic yet insightful moment, Mr. Roberts offered a very distinc-tive image defining the boundary between company management and the board of directors:

> The perfect board member practices the principle of NIFO—nose in, fingers out. It's the job of management to run the business. The board is there to stick its nose into the business and make sure everything is according to plan without being too hands-on. (Cox 2010)

Because transformations are particularly susceptible to unanticipated issues and disruptions, the concept of NIFO is a critical consideration in achieving success.

As we have been discussing, the work of the company leadership, the workforce, and the oversight provided through the board and indepen-dent reviews is what collectively ensures the success of the transformation project. If any of the three components is missing or not equally engaged, the success of the transformation is jeopardized.

Projects in which any of these three components is minimalized can readily find itself facing issues reminiscent of those we saw with the National Institutes of Health (Chapter 2), with the Department of Homeland Security's attempt to create a virtual fence (Chapter 3), with the Champlain Bridge Project (Chapter 4), or, as in the beginning of this chapter, the undoing of RadioShack.

Running a transformation project requires the right set of tools and techniques underpinned by the commitment, expertise, and experience of a capable company leadership, a talented and resourceful workforce, and an informed and engaged board of directors. It is only the talent of all three agencies involved—making use of the tools and techniques we have been discussing—that ultimately positions the company for and delivers a successful transformation.

It is this same set of resources and commitment, as will be discussed in Chapter 6, that is the essential ingredient in the final transitioning and transforming of the company from its previous reality into its new incarnation.

CHAPTER 6

Delivering the Transformed Company

But the fact is, Mr. Chairman, for all the challenges the Postal Service of the 21st century faces, it still retains its traditional place as a key cog in how American businesses conduct their affairs and how Americans all across this land communicate.

—John M. McHugh, 21st Secretary of the Army
Testimony before Committee on Homeland Security and
Governmental Affairs, November 15, 2016

In the year before the American Revolution, the Continental Congress established a postal system and named Benjamin Franklin as the first postmaster general. Given the postal service's key role in binding the colonies and then the states together, the post office was understood to be integral to the nation's political aspirations, so much so that beginning with Andrew Jackson's administration, postmasters general served as members of the President's Cabinet. The nature of postal services went on largely unchanged during the intervening years until the 1960s when services began to suffer owing to aging facilities and equipment, wage and management issues, and an increasing reliance on subsidized postage rates.

Recognizing a change was essential, President Nixon signed into law the Postal Reorganization Act of 1970, restructuring the postal system into an "independent establishment of the executive branch" run by an 11-member board of governors (9 presidential appointees, the postmaster general, and the deputy postmaster general). Consistent with this new relative degree of independence, the postal service was also charged with a break-even financial mandate.

At the same time, while preserving certain protections for the postal service, the Law, in addition to subjecting the service to extensive government review through several congressional oversight bodies, also created the Postal Rate Commission, which requires public administrative hearings before rates can be changed. Despite the vast changes introduced by the Law, the fundamental service expectation remained; often referred to as the postal service's "Universal Service Mission," the obligation remained for it to provide mail service to "Everyone, Everywhere, Every Day."

Three decades later, as service again began to falter, in February 2002, a General Accounting Office report expressed an urgent need for a transformation: "The Postal Service's basic business model ... is increasingly problematic since mail volume could stagnate or decline further, and the Postal Service has difficulty in making and sustaining productivity increases" (GAO 2002). In response, in April of that year, John E. Potter, the postmaster general at the time, delivered a 500+-page Transformation Plan to Congress.

In the very first paragraph of the Executive Summary, the postal service acknowledged the depth of its difficulties:

> We live in challenging times. Long-term technological and commercial trends, often termed the Second Industrial Revolution, are fundamentally reshaping national and international services for collection, transport, and delivery of all types of postal products. These trends will compel a fundamental transformation in our national approach toward the postal service as an institution and the delivery services sector as a whole. (U.S. Postal Service [USPS] 2002)

While the Postal Reorganization Act had steadied the post office's performance for more than 30 years, the plan could not anticipate the challenges being experienced in 2002:

Changing customer needs: The postal service was ill-equipped to meet "increasingly varied customer requirements."

Eroding mail volumes: Electronic alternatives to mail, such as online payments, represented direct and substantial challenges to first-class mail.

Rising costs: Despite productivity enhancements gained from automation, the costs of maintaining the infrastructure as well as an ever-expanding postal network (including worker benefits) were rising faster than revenue.

Expansive competition: Foreign postal services, global parcel services, and express delivery businesses were increasingly penetrating what had been an exclusive Postal Service market.

Increasing security concerns: The demands for increased information security were requiring expensive investments in controls and equipment.

As the Transformation Plan anticipated, over the coming years, the postal service experienced a decline of more than 50 billion pieces of mail due to electronic diversion, the economic recession, and changing customer needs; at the same time, mail was being provided to more than 10 million additional delivery points. Despite the reduction in the volume of mail and the increases in delivery sites, as noted in its 2017–2021 Strategic Plan, during this period the postal service was able to achieve total revenue growth (USPS n.d.).

This growth, envisioned in the Transformation Plan and implemented through a succession of strategic plans, comes as a consequence of transforming operations and services: redesigning postal networks, realigning and right-sizing the workforce, modifying post office hours, deploying new technologies, expanding delivery windows, and increasing alternative access for services. In recognition of the magnitude and breadth of the transformation, the postal service was recognized in an industry-wide assessment as the most efficient mail service among major industrialized countries.

Because in this chapter we want to review the predicates of the transformation process and then explain the final steps in readying to open the doors to your newly transformed company, we thought it fit—in contrast to the examples provided at the beginning of our preceding chapters—to use this chapter to highlight what has been independently recognized as a well-administered and successful transformation (Jackson, Druck, and Albury 2016).

So, before summarizing some of the attributes that made transformation of the U.S. Postal Service successful, let's examine a broader perspective of the transformation process and then address the concluding steps in transitioning to the operational new business entity—the two interconnected components that together deliver the transformed company (Figure 6.1).

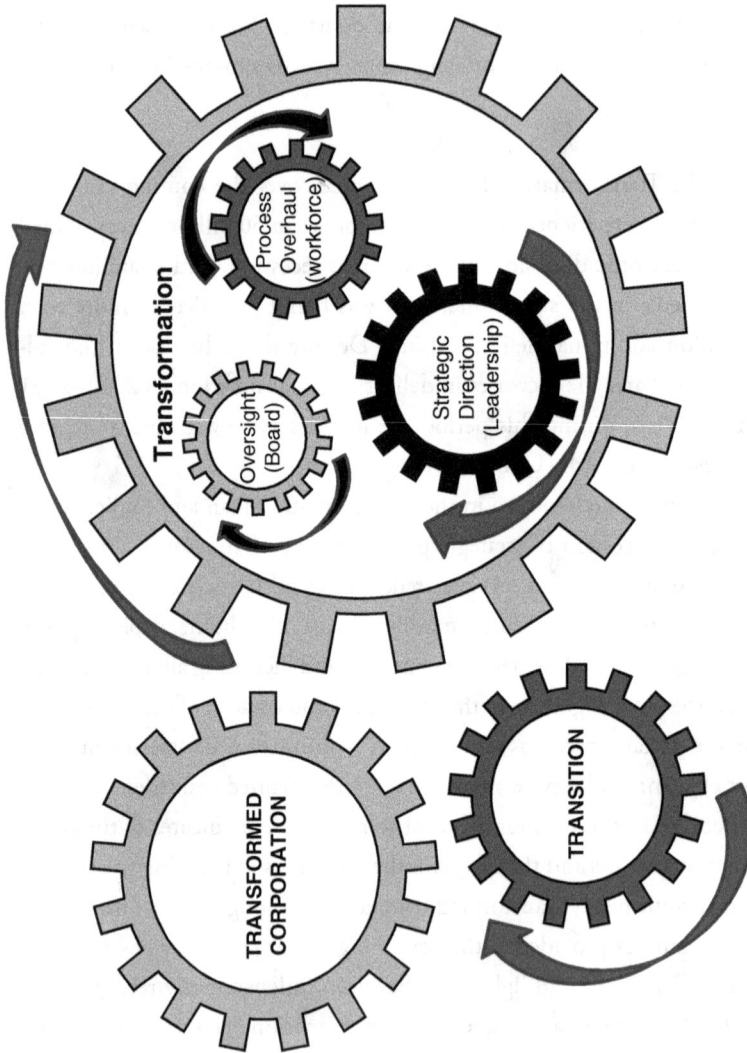

Figure 6.1 *Delivering the transformed corporation*

The gears in the figure are labeled:

- Process Overhaul (workforce)
- Oversight (Board)
- Strategic Direction (Leadership)
- Transformation
- TRANSFORMED CORPORATION
- TRANSITION

The Transformation Process: A Broadened Perspective

Having examined the various mechanics associated with completing the transformation in the preceding chapters, we can take a moment to re-examine and reiterate the essence of the transformation from a widened perspective and also to use this examination to reiterate some of the key points, principles, and central attributes of an effective transformation.

Stated in the most generalized manner, a successful transformation effort is a consequence of two factors: (1) an integrated and committed team, and (2) an appreciation of the values and expectations the team is seeking to deliver.

The Team

As we have been discussing, the process of transformation has many parts and several critical contributors. After all of the entities involved in corporate decision making have had some input and buy-in as to whether or not a company needs to transform itself, the question becomes, "where do we start?" As we have asserted, the answer to that question is at the top—with those individuals in charge of leading the business.

After the executive leadership has been mobilized and the transformation is underway, it is essential to know where the organization stands financially. Often, strategy begins with an overall financial objective, such as "return on investment" or capital. Yet, financial goals may not be enough; leadership needs to develop a strategy that enables the business to adapt quickly to new and potentially unfamiliar initiatives. In most situations this would equate to understanding, improving, and simplifying processes and infrastructure to position the business to be more agile. As is evident, to be successful, this activity must involve the engagement of everyone in the company, requiring them to participate wholeheartedly, to think differently, and to rely as much on creativity as on experience and expertise.

It is not enough to create objectives that meet the needs of organizational improvements. A holistic transformation will have to address financial objectives that will satisfy shareholders; meet the needs and expectations of the customers; identify critical business processes; and evaluate and ensure availability of every resource necessary to equip the organization. Success is predicated on having the wherewithal to optimize and improve on the critical processes coupled with the motivated personnel to make it happen.

It's only once the entire corporate community is engaged that the focus shifts to use of the tools we have shared to translate the resulting strategic objectives into tangible terms supported by tools to communicate that set of expectations throughout the chain of command extending from the front office to the shop floor.

Central to the transformation's success is recognizing the depth of engagement required. The biggest shifts in day-to-day activities fall not to the leadership team but, rather, to the line management and the workers on the shop floor, in the field, and in the administrative offices. Engagement and development of the workforce represents the bedrock upon which the transformed company is founded. Building upon the capabilities of those employees, enhancing their ownership of redesigned processes, and intensifying their confidence in the new assignments they have inherited will, ultimately, make or break the transformation.

Motivating these communities is a function not only of a reasonable recognition and reward systems; it is underpinned by a set of metrics—or performance indicators—that form the basis for regular evaluations of progress. The value of those evaluations is a function of identifying performance indicators of immediate relevance to the transformation's strategic objectives. For example, in the pre-transformed company structure, a metric used in the warehouse might have measured on-time receipt of critical replacement parts; in the process of transforming the company, the warehouse metric may need to pertain to shelf space made available through elimination of materials no longer needed by the redesigned processes.

Because of the evolving transformation, all metrics need to be periodically re-evaluated to ensure they continue to align with the progress toward completing strategic objectives. Updating metrics not only serves to allow employees to gage progress (and potentially earn incentives), it is also a strong indicator of precisely how well first and second line management understand the overall plan and are engaged in monitoring the transformation and in delivering on the expectations for their respective departments.

As we have discussed previously, there is also one more critical component of the team: the board of directors. From their vantage point, they have a duty to monitor and provide oversight of the transformation—from inception through completion. It is their professional obligation to provide the oversight that allows them to observe, monitor, and—if necessary—challenge the corporate leadership.

The board's responsibility extends from ensuring that the commitment to the transformation is maintained to monitoring that the flow of expectations, the overall strategy, and the supporting objectives are consistently communicated throughout the entire organization. In that way, indirectly, the board confirms that exercises, objectives, meetings, and communication plans are given careful attention by the leadership.

Its role, largely achieved through utilization of independent review teams, holds leadership accountable for more than simply monitoring and reporting on performance; rather, leadership is expected to be held accountable for delivering the transformation on schedule and on budget. This responsibility requires the board to be attuned to recognizing leadership's abilities and practices relative to taking decisive action, providing direction, identifying and eliminating distractions, communicating effectively, and motivating all levels of the organization.

Monitoring is essential throughout the transformation. In some instances, the primary leadership capabilities that made an executive successful in the company prior to its transformation may not be the same set of skills needed for leading the transformation or, subsequently, for leading the transformed company. In such instances—as was demonstrated in the unraveling of RadioShack—failure to maintain the leadership, particularly the CEO, with the right skills can result in a less-than-satisfactory transformation and less-than-satisfactory corporate performance.

Values and Expectations

Transformations are inherently challenging. In a *Forbes* magazine article entitled "Four Steps to a Successful Business Transformation," Robert T. Vanderwerf, the Transformation Strategy Leader for KPMG (a multinational professional services network), offered the following insightful summation of the challenge: "We are living in interesting times, with multiple transformation triggers all present at the same time, all equally intense.

When four or five significant drivers are changing at the same time, the business environment becomes highly complex" (Moreno 2014).

Given the complexity, no single individual can presume to have all of the answers. Based on the size and dimension of the transformation, a phased approach may be in order to allow opportunities and challenges to unfold so as to maintain a steady course during the transformation. In the near term, substantial improvements in efficiency may be accomplished without major revisions to the core business; then, as the pathway becomes more defined, these preliminary changes can be accompanied by the fundamental restructuring of the organizational framework and by strategic market positioning.

The point is that it is critical to conduct a transformation in a manner that is fitted to the new and modern business model to be forged, while at the same time preparing the management team and organizational staff to manage the upcoming changes effectively, without impact on continuity of ongoing work activity.

A key factor in moving to the new model is the responsibility to maintain financial viability while completing the range of transformation tasks and activities. To accomplish this end, the team must remain constantly vigilant and remain attentive to three principal factors:

- Promoting growth through increased value of products and services
- Improving operational efficiency
- Enhancing the performance-based culture

Added Value and Flexibility

The primary consideration is ensuring that the analysis encompasses the entire spectrum of products and services offered to the existing and future consumer/client base. The transformation must offer flexible options that meet stakeholder expectations, fulfill client requirements, and create value added to the end user. The organization should find ways to use existing resources to identify efficiencies, which can offset anticipated losses from the implementation of long lead time initiatives. The objective should be to nurture an environment that is flexible enough to adapt to change. To accomplish this goal, the leadership can take a variety of actions:

- Introduce less expensive/more timely access to products and services
- Collect data that assist in analyzing product and process improvements and that assist in identifying process and production weaknesses
- Promote enhancements in the supply chain, including potential outsourcing of noncritical activities
- Expand existing revenue sources—leverage assets, infrastructure, and intellectual properties
- Routinely solicit feedback and suggestions from customers
- Encourage workers to identify new product lines and enhanced services
- Support a robust employee retention and development program

Operational Efficiency

Cost containment is often the most important customer-focused strategy, especially for large businesses that rely heavily on existing infrastructure. It is difficult to control costs when volume declines while the infrastructure costs remain stagnant or are rising. Even when costs are well controlled, cost savings should be aggressively pursued. Numerous candidates for operational efficiency should be regularly explored:

- Involve a broad spectrum of workers in benchmarking
- Standardize best practices within each organization from production to finance
- Integrate formal planning and scheduling tools at all organizational levels
- Consider novel employment actions—work sharing, telecommuting
- Provide training in LEAN, Six Sigma, and other productivity assessment/enhancement techniques
- Develop alternative purchasing strategies—for example, just-in-time delivery vs. warehousing
- As appropriate, create collaborative sessions with oversight, regulatory, and government agencies to identify mutually beneficial opportunities for streamlining work processes

Performance-Driven Culture

As part of the transformation, breakthrough productivity initiatives will be achievable only if significant progress in encouraging a performance-based culture is achieved—a culture that communicates an interest in the performance and the well-being of the workforce. Leadership is charged with creating and sustaining an effective, diverse, and motivated workforce whose members know what is expected of them and who are recognized for individual and team accomplishments. The challenge is to assure continuity at all levels of the corporation, including during the transformation.

To address the challenge, consider implementing some of the following programs:

- Design recruitment strategies targeting critical disciplines and work groups
- Complete periodic succession planning that concentrates on promoting internal candidates in conjunction with defining and monitoring candidate preparations and qualifications of high-potential candidates
- Maintain training and development programs that address all levels of workers and provide for diverse learning styles (e.g., classroom, online, hands-on field training)
- Make metrics a formal part of the decision-making regime: evaluating metric effectiveness, holding periodic review meetings to evaluate performance, and holding owners accountable
- Reinforce an expectation regarding the integrity of the work environment: safety, security, respectful interactions
- Optimize utilization of worker skills and talents through promotion opportunities, rotational assignments, and developmental training

As is suggested by the preceding lists of considerations, transformations need to be treated like a project and managed accordingly. Appointing a qualified project manager to oversee transitional activities is central to ensuring that the organizational activities remain on track and that those assigned activities have the resources and technical guidance necessary to complete the tasks identified. In addition, the project manager for the transformation should be provided not only with the responsibility for ensuring that reviews and actions are implemented, but must be given authority to take actions as may be necessary to maintain costs, accelerate schedules, and be immediately and personally responsive to unanticipated distractions.

A successful transformation is—when examined from this broadened perspective—an amalgamation of a number of contributing factors: well-defined values and expectations, flexibility in responding to challenges, attention to operational efficiency, and a performance-driven culture. Only when all these factors are working well, when the mechanics of transformation are attended to in a disciplined fashion and complemented by an effective oversight program, is the company positioned to shift to the final preparations to open the doors of the newly transformed company. This is the stage at which transformation enters the transition phase.

The Transition Process

Most companies get the vision right, but the execution is the hard part. In our current working environments, organizations almost always underestimate the effort and resources necessary to successfully implement significant changes to their existing operating model, and want to shortcut operating model changes necessary to make the final transition to welcoming customers to the suite of transformed products and services. In this stage, again, there is need for a rigorous assessment of the readiness of people, processes, technology, and management systems.

In summary, the transition process concentrates on the following objectives:

- Minimize or avoid impacts to continuity of operations
- Identify key issues and pursue them through complete resolution
- Identify roles and responsibilities for completing all remaining actions (including any punch-list items carried forward into this period)
- Determine required interactions with any agencies/offices that require signoff before the business opens (e.g., business licenses, inspections)

- Document all final review/readiness requirements, including a
  schedule of all remaining activities, any internal reviews, and final
  validations

Implementing the transition is best accomplished through the development of a preliminary transition plan followed by the development of a final transition plan. The preliminary transition plan should include a description of a transition management approach and structure, a description of transition activities broken down by major work elements, a preliminary execution schedule, and a high-level resource loading of the activities. In particular, the plan should provide sufficient detail regarding:

- Identification of preliminary transition ideas
- Development of a preliminary transition schedule
- Design of a communication plan and communication strategy
- Preliminary realignment of organizational structure (if necessary)
- Refinement of an initial transition staffing plan

The primary objectives of this plan are (1) to ensure that everyone has agreed to the fundamental objectives of what needs to happen, (2) to provide a reference point for those being introduced to the post-transformation process and environment, and (3) to identify potential benchmarking activities.

As such, the preliminary transition plan should be utilized as a roadmap for the detailed initiatives and improvement opportunities that each functional/project organization will provide at a later date. Every transition team member should have an understanding about the strategic and transformative vision. Stated simply, the preliminary transition plan is the resource tool that offers all individuals assurance that they are contributors to both the vision and to the transformation.

Once the preliminary transition plan has been developed, it should be circulated within the management team to ensure that it captures the essence of the transformation direction; this review, in turn, constitutes the basis for generating the final transition plan. This final version of the plan further details the nature and responsibility for any remaining actions, giving attention to the specific tasks pertaining to finalizing the readiness of each individual company department. In comparison, the draft plan issued previously concentrates on global issues—matters of significance to the company as a whole that need to be addressed jointly across multiple organizations in readying the company for preparation to proceed to finite, localized tasks.

The transition plan also incorporates organizationally specific transition plans that break down the company's strategic transformative initiatives into actions more specific and applicable to each function or operation. In so doing, the process creates a new baseline that reflects all tasks. Activities and status from each organization should be captured on activity sheets and used to track and assess transition progress/status. The activity sheets should also be used to identify emerging tasks, identify issues for management resolution, and provide the basis for substantive communication with all transition staff. Accordingly, the transition plan should include:

- Review of existing project, program, and management system documents
- Lists of any actions not completed since the issuance of the draft plan, along with the indication of who is responsible to complete the action and by what date
- A gap analysis between the existing processes and the proposed strategic initiatives
- Actions needed to align individual program initiatives with the leadership's vision
- Means to measure and document progress and completion of all remaining actions

Also, if not already implemented, this phase should review organizational recommendations, implementing procedures, staffing projections, longer-term objectives to be considered for streamlining processes, and minimizing of organizational interfaces. Having an integrated management approach, including a resource-loaded schedule for performing project deliverables and services, will also be important from the standpoint of maintaining financial accountability and for keeping stakeholders and the board of directors informed. (Figure 6.2 encapsulates the principal components of the transition phase.)

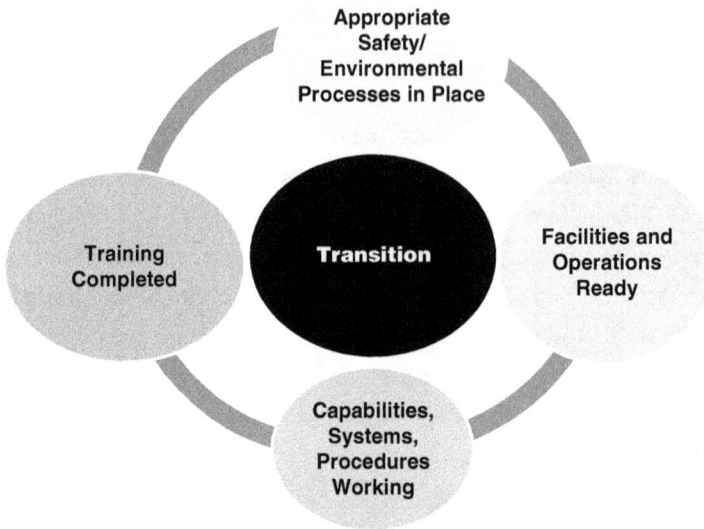

Figure 6.2 Fundamentals of transitioning the transformed company

Project Commissioning

Project commissioning is the last component to a successful transition. This stage, closely linked with the transition phase, concludes with the final documentation that all aspects of the transformation are complete, the integration of components has been achieved, and the system and production capabilities have been demonstrated as consistent with the fundamental expectations of the transformation. Essentially, project commissioning is the final check that all systems are prepared to perform as planned and at a commercial rate of production. Given this coordination between transitioning and project commission, the individual who served as the project manager for the transition should be retained as the lead for the project commissioning phase.

This phase, in large extent, is a reversal of the planning phase of the transformation. Whereas the planning effort proceeded through a sequence of steps leading from the development of the expectations through delivery, project commissioning addresses the same components of the transformation but begins with assessing readiness of the personnel and then working back to the identification of requirements and the process employed for establishing the expectations for the project. This sequence allows each element to be viewed and assessed independently, avoiding the potential for noncritical thinking, anchoring, or confirmation biases (Figure 6.3).

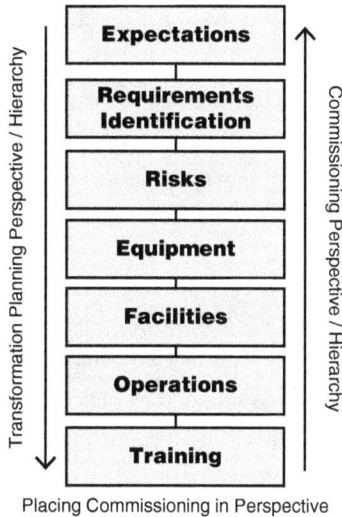

Placing Commissioning in Perspective

Figure 6.3 The relationship between planning and project commissioning

In this final stage, all activities and findings are recorded on datasheets and checklists that, once all have been completed, are compiled for review by the project manager—and, if requested—by the board of directors. The final review and approval by the project manager and/or board of directors is the official stamp that the newly transformed business is ready to open its doors.

Doing It Right

Given this overview of the expectations for a successful transformation and delivery of the transformed company, let's momentarily return to the discussion of the U.S. Postal Service's transformation. Reviewing the process and practices of the postal service will help provide a tangible illustration of a well-orchestrated transformation and a practical demonstration of foundational principles we have been discussing throughout this text.

In summary, the U.S. Postal Service was successful owing to diligently and thoroughly proceeding through the following sequence:

- Assessing the perceived challenges that precipitated the transformation effort
- Soliciting feedback as a basis for developing reasonable customer expectations
- Conducting a thorough analysis of the business foundations
- Translating expectations into tangible actions
- Following through utilizing multiple, actionable implementation plans

Assessing Challenges

As noted by the postmaster general in the 2002 Transformation Plan, "We have to come to grips with the reality that the legislation that created the postal service more than 30 years ago now puts us out of step with our customers, our competitors, and the marketplace." As he succinctly noted, "In a number of possible future scenarios, the Postal Service may soon find itself increasingly ill-equipped to serve the postal needs of the nation."

For postal service successful transformation was, in large measure, a result of their conscientious focus on five principal challenges:

- Changing customer needs
- Eroding mail volumes
- Rising costs
- Expansive competition
- Increasing security concerns

To address these challenges, the postal service first undertook an exhaustive campaign to ascertain just what those changing customer needs were and how customers perceived of future needs for postal services.

Soliciting Customer Input

The postal service began by designing and documenting the framework for its transformation. Following the strategy laid out in its Outline for Discussion: Concepts for Postal Transformation, the postal service placed notices in the

Federal Register soliciting comments, followed by issuing web-based communications, conducting surveys distributed by mail, and holding a series of focus groups and panel discussions. In addition, the process of soliciting feedback included congressional hearings, a national telephone survey, and a questionnaire issued to postal executives (Table 6.1) (USPS 2001).

Table 6.1 Maximizing customer input

Stakeholder Community	Input Mechanism	Detail	Themes Discussed
General retail customers	Survey	2,000+ interviews conducted	• Business environment
	Online comments	~150 comments received	• Cultural transformation
	Focus groups	14 sessions held	• Customer service • Human Resources
Major corporate users	Board of governor panel sessions	Meetings with six high-volume corporate customers	• Improved core services
			• Labor relations
Employees	Board of governors panel sessions with unions and management associations	Sessions with six postal labor/management representatives	• Mail safety • Mission and goals • New products and services • Postal operations
Postal executives	Postal Service Executive Survey	250+ surveys completed	• Postal privatization • Postal
Suppliers	Meetings with postal Supplier Quality Council	Two meetings, attended by 20 supplier representatives	transformation • Productivity • Public perception
Policy makers	Comments solicited through Federal Register	Position paper drafted; congressional hearings held	• Rates and pricing • Regulatory reform • Stakeholder education
Commercial mail companies	Meetings with Mailers Technical Advisory Committee	Meetings held with 170 mailing industry association representatives	• Universal service

The solicitations and interactive sessions focused on nine central questions:

- What should America's postal system be like (or transformed into) in the next decade?
- Should America's postal system provide universal service, and what should that service entail?

As a government agency, the postal service would concentrate more on its role as an essential government service—similar to the national park system, and would not concern itself with markets adequately addressed by the private sector. Given the likely elimination of services, the concept of universal service would no longer apply. As a privatized corporation, the postal service could potentially provide universal service, but most likely major services would be subcontracted; implementing market-based pricing would necessarily require staffing reductions and service limitations. In comparison, transitioning to a commercial government enterprise would place the postal service on a business-like footing, offering traditional and nontraditional products and services based on market-based pricing.

Given the breadth of its analysis of the challenges and the extensive stakeholder input to the process, the postal service was well-equipped to reach a decisive and reasoned decision regarding the most appropriate business model. Acknowledging the stakeholder input along with the institution's historic and enduring core values, vision, and mission, the board of governors and senior leadership of the postal service concluded that a commercial government enterprise offered "the best hope for transforming the Postal Service into an enterprise equipped to maintain universal service at affordable prices in the economy of the 21st century."

Translating Expectations into Actions

Having taken into account the challenges engendering the transformation, the customer expectations, and the design of the new business model, the postal service defined actions relative to a broad base of transformative actions enumerated within two, principal "imperatives": (1) foster growth through customer value, and (2) expand access to post services. From these imperatives, a set of actions were derived addressing all facets of the postal service's responsibilities and services: Actions proposed represented extensive transformations in customer service and satisfaction; automation, technology, and process redesign; cost reductions; improved utilization of people, equipment, and facilities; labor and employment reforms; improved supply chain management; regulatory and legislative reform; and pricing and postal rate controls.

A few select examples of the actions identified should suggest the extent of proposed redefinition:

- Develop "intelligent mail"—products tracked throughout processing and delivery
- Streamline supply chain processes
- Reduce the time letter carriers spend in the post office
- Implement planning, routing, and tracking programs to reduce transportation costs
- Introduce more self-service options (e.g., secure kiosks offering multiple services)
- Optimize logistics networks (e.g., number and location of processing centers, transportation modes, and delivery routes)
- Improve performance monitoring by implementing data-driven assessment tools
- Move repetitive transactional work to a shared services environment
- Improve the collective bargaining and arbitration processes
- Develop tools to enhance personnel recruiting and retention
- Introduce greater flexibility and predictability in setting and adjusting postal rates.

Following through Utilizing Multiple, Actionable Implementation Plans

Having developed a path forward in 2002, the postal service pushed forward with its planned actions. In September 2005, the postal service published its Strategic Transformation Plan 2006–2010 to build "on the momentum of our original Transformation Plan" to stay "focused on our core business and the strategies we know produce results," and to document how "the Postal Service has delivered on its promise of focus and results."

As the 2006–2010 strategic plan pointed out, in the intervening years since the issuance of the 2002 Transformation Plan, more than 80,000 jobs had been reduced; a cumulative savings of approximately $13 billion had been achieved; the postal service was delivering twice as much mail as it had been delivering, but had not needed to increase staffing. Relying

- What should the core service of the future postal service be?
- How should the nation structure a future postal system to ensure it is productive and efficient?
- Can the postal service continue to provide universal service under the current financial arrangements? Are there other financing mechanisms needed?
- What steps should be taken to anticipate future human capital requirements?
- Is there a commercially oriented structure that would still provide universal coverage?
- How should a privately owned postal entity or entities perform?
- Are there other models that may do a better job for the American people?

Conducting a thorough Analysis of the Business Foundations

The hallmark of a transformation, as we have noted, is in challenging the corporation's foundational elements. Strategic transformation, as we have been asserting, represents a total rethinking of what the company is, what it does, who its customer base is, and where it is going. In keeping with our methodology, this willingness to re-evaluate its central core was a key component of the postal service transformation.

As was recognized in the Transformation Plan, the changes needed to maintain the postal service's long-term viability demanded not only re-thinking processes, but, rather, necessitated fundamental restructuring of the legislative and regulatory framework. The postal service's examination of challenges "illuminated important issues, many of which raise implications that stretch beyond legislative remedies."

At its most fundamental basis, moving forward required a careful and deliberative evaluation of three distinctively different business models for the postal service: (1) a government agency focused on providing services not adequately provided in the commercial market, operating with continued support of government subsidies; (2) a privatized corporation—a commercial business entity with private shareholders; or (3) a commercial government enterprise—a government-owned enterprise operating commercially in the market to provide postal and related services.

on the same basic goals as cited in the 2002 plan, the 2006–2010 plan laid out four primary strategic goals continuing and complementing the work begun by the 2002 plan—generate revenue, reduce costs, engage employees, and improve service. These goals, in turn, were proposed to be fulfilled by four "transformation strategies":

- Create more customer value with products and services: Incorporating technology and leveraging assets to transform product offerings by making them easier to use and better tailoring them to the needs of specific customers. As example, the postal service introduced a commercial service using barcodes to track first-class mail, periodicals, and standard mail through every stage of the processing and delivery processes.

- Customize and simplify pricing: Using the appropriate regulatory processes to customize prices to meet the needs of business customers. As example, the postal service pioneered Negotiated Service Agreements to customize prices for large volume mailers.

- Enhance access and ease of use: By taking advantage of the power of the Internet and the reach of its delivery network, the postal service provided customers with access to new products and services. For example, the postal service introduced Click-N-Ship, which allowed customers to print postage and labels online, and also made good on its plan to implement Automated Postal Center kiosks providing an alternative to counter services.

- Make aggressive sales, promotions, and outreach: Equipping the entire workforce of 700,000 employees to work together and reach out to customers to grow business for the postal service. For example, the postal service launched "Branding through the Mailbox," a marketing campaign that set the postal service as a strategic partner in assisting customers in developing effective direct mail campaigns (USPS 2005).

From their origins in the 2002 Transformation Plan, the initiatives continued to be enhanced, updated, and complemented. As summarized in the most recent of the strategic plans implementing the 2002-originated changes, the postal service's strategic plan for the years 2017–2021 offers this concluding statement committing to continued transformation of the postal service business model and its products and services:

> Deeper partnerships with customers, suppliers, and the mailing industry will improve the quality of mail and service delivery. In addition, the Postal Service will continue to develop pricing incentives and invest in platforms that reinforce efficiency and service improvement. Our mission is an important one—exemplified by more than 240 years of service to the American people. We strive to continue to transform the Postal Service to not merely adapt to ever-changing customer needs but to anticipate, prepare for, and implement solutions as a leader in the industry—Future Ready. (USPS n.d.)

Conclusion

Transformation is an ongoing process. In order to be sustainable, every business, organization, and institutional entity must periodically take a moment of pause, and look at its existing business model without prejudice. If the existing business model is not sustainable, a transformation might be in order.

Great business leaders understand how important it is to reinvest in the company whether it be equipment, infrastructure, and/or human capital, but it is just as important to invest in a sustainable vision that is created by the trusted leadership in an organization. Some industries can support rapid growth and transformation on a daily basis. Their business model is built on quick decision making, regrouping, and redirection at the signs of potential market impacts. However, most organizations—especially large corporations that are reliant on well-ingrained and codified practices and protocols—might take a conservative approach and be less immediately receptive to change and transformation.

However, even in the most conservative of business environments, the real debate is not one between whether or not to transform in response to corporate triggers; to survive in an environment of constant disruption, the only practical decision is a matter of the pace by which transformation will be allowed to proceed. The key to having a successful transformation and strategic direction is to recognize the pace in which your organization can successfully implement change. There is such a thing as acting too soon, pressing too hard, and forcing an idea and/or change that is premature. Having the ability to work within, or just on the periphery, of what can be recognized as the transitional comfort zone is essential to ensuring that there will be an open discussion and buy-in to a necessary transformation that will ensure sustainability. Of course, as we have sought to make evident, the consequence of being too slow and unwilling to transform is to jeopardize the company's financial health and future.

Our advice on transformation is that there is always room for improvement. The timeline for undergoing that transformation must be supported by and aligned with the business model. If you are to be the agent of change, the individual who sees the transformative vision long before there is even a whisper of solidarity toward the idea, it is important to recognize your eventual contribution toward the ultimate success of what might evolve out of your desire to recognize organizational success.

If the company (its workforce, leadership, and board of directors) is not given to immediate enterprise-wide redefinition, step-wise improvements can be introduced: implementing a better defined organizational structure, completing a requirements review, leveraging resources to establish better financial positioning, enhancing the performance-based culture, bringing on new technology, encouraging greater attention to performance monitoring and performance efficiency.

Use the transformation process we have shared to revisit good ideas, implement best practices, stretch boundaries, and expand the current cultural mindset. Identify immediate improvements, influence management teams, proactively present your long-term ideas, and circulate these ideas among others.

In the end, it is the combination of a clear vision and an effective team that will deliver your company's transformation (Figure 6.4). In this text you have the tools and the processes; all you need to add in order to conduct a successful transformation is the commitment!

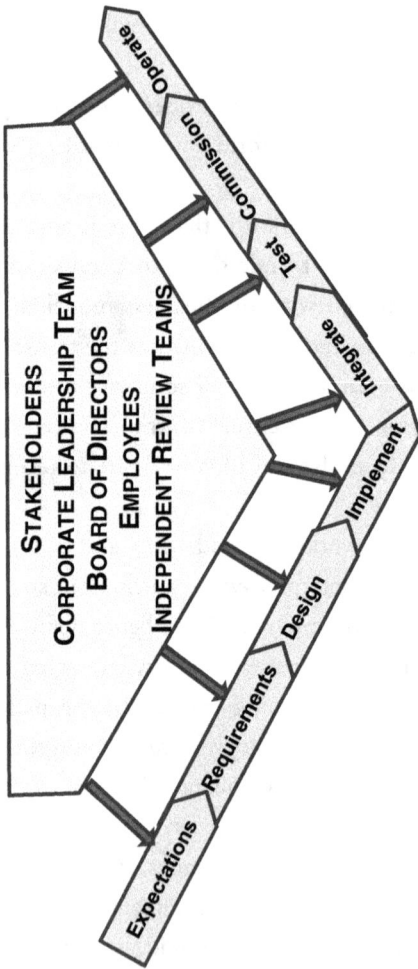

Figure 6.4 The collaborative delivery of a successful transformation

References

Introduction

Anthony, S.D, P. Viguerie, E.I. Schwartz, and J. Van Landeghem. February, 2018. "2018 Corporate Longevity Forecast: Creative Destruction Is Accelerating," *Innosight*. https://www.innosight.com/wp-content/uploads/2017/11/Innosight-Corporate-Longevity-2018.pdf, (accessed September 2019).

Ferguson, D. n.d. "Therbligs: The Keys to Simplifying Work," *The Gilbreth Network*. http://gilbrethnetwork.tripod.com/therbligs.html, (accessed March 2019).

"If Japan Can, Why Can't We?" n.d. *NBC News White Paper*. http://www.youtube.com/watch?v=vcG_Pmt_Ny4, (accessed April 2019).

Taylor, F.W. 1947. *Scientific Management, Comprising Shop Management: The Principles of Scientific Management and Testimony before the Special House Committee*. New York, NY: Harper & Brothers.

Chapter 1

Anthony, S.D, P. Viguerie, E.I. Schwartz, and J. Van Landeghem. February, 2018. "2018 Corporate Longevity Forecast: Creative Destruction is Accelerating," *Innosight*. https://www.innosight.com/wp-content/uploads/2017/11/Innosight-Corporate-Longevity-2018.pdf, (accessed September 2019).

Gilbert, C., M. Evring, and R.N. Foster. December, 2012. "Two Routes to Resilience," *Harvard Business Review*. https://hbr.org/2012/12/two-routes-to-resilience

Chapter 2

Champion-Awwad, O., A. Hayton, L. Smith, and M. Vuaran. 2014. "The National Program for IT in the NHS: A Case History," *MPhil Public Policy*. University of Cambridge.

Dewey, J. 1910. *How We Think*. New York, NY: B.C. Heath & Co.

Fayol, H. 1949. *General and Industrial Administration*. London, UK: Sir Isaac Pitman & Sons.

Gavetti, G., and J.W. Rivkin. 2005. "How Strategists Really Think: Tapping Power of Analogy." *Harvard Business Review*, pp. 54-65.

Mintzberg, H. 1990. "The Manager's Job: Folklore and Fact." *Harvard Business Review*, pp. 163-76.

Rouse, W.B. 2005. "A Theory of Enterprise Transformation." *Systems Engineering* 8, pp. 279-95.

Webster, F.J. Jr. 2009. "Marketing IS Management: The Wisdom of Peter Drucker." *Journal of the Academy of Marketing Science* 37, pp. 20-27.

Chapter 3

U.S. Department of Energy. 1984. *Cost and Schedule Control Systems Criteria for Contract Performance Measurements, DOE MA/-0155*. Guidance Document. Washington, DC: U. S. Department of Energy. https://www.osti.gov/servlets/purl/7044511

U.S. General Accounting Office. 2006. *Border Security: Key Unresolved Issues Justify Reevaluation of Border Surveillance Technology Program.* GAO-06-295. Washington, DC: U.S. GAO. https://www.gao.gov/assets/250/249053.pdf

U.S. General Accounting Office. 2008. *Secure Border Initiative: DHS Needs to Address Significant Risks in Delivering Key Technology Investment.* GAO-08-1086. Washington, DC: U.S. GAO. https://www.gao.gov/new.items/d081086.pdf

U.S. General Accounting Office. 2009. *Secure Border Initiative: Technology Development Delays Persis and the Impact of Border Fencing Hand Not Been Assessed.* GAO-09-1013T. Washington, DC: U.S. GAO. https://www.gao.gov/new.items/d091013t.pdf

U.S. General Accounting Office. 2010a. *Secure Border Initiative: DHS Needs to Reconsider Its Proposed Investment in Key Technology Program.* GAO-10-340. Washington, DC: U.S. GAO. https://www.gao.gov/assets/310/304036.pdf

U.S. General Accounting Office. 2010b. *Secure Border Initiative: DH Needs to Strengthen Management and Oversight of Its Prime Contractor.* GAO-11-16. Washington, DC: U.S. GAO. https://www.gao.gov/assets/320/311431.pdf

Chapter 4

The Canadian Press. April 20, 2011. "Say Your Prayers As You Cross the Champlain Bridge," *CTV News.* https://montreal.ctvnews.ca/say-your-prayers-as-you-cross-the-champlain-bridge-1.634107.

The Canadian Press. n.d. "Montreal's New Samual De Champlain Bridge Official Inaugurated," *The Globe and Mail.* https://www.theglobeandmail.com/news/national/champlain-bridge-is-falling-down-montreal-pays-for-past-penny-pinching/article15699180, (accessed June 28, 2019).

CBC News. October 19, 2016. "Highway 15 Overpass, Completed Last Year, Now Being Demolished," *CBC News.* https://www.cbc.ca/news/canada/montreal/montreal-highway-15-overpass-torn-down-1.3811421.

CTV News.ca Staff. October 20, 2016. "Brand New $11-Million Overpass Torn Down in Montreal," *CTV News.* https://www.ctvnews.ca/canada/brand-new-11-milion-overpass-torn-down-in-montreal-1.3123375, (accessed June 2019).

Field, A. May 3, 2014. "6 Ways to Foster Collaboration in Your Workplace," *Entrepreneurship.* https://www.under30ceo.com/6-ways-foster-collaboration-workplace.

Gohier, P. August 23, 2011. "Montreal Is Falling Down," *Macleans.* https://www.macleans.ca/news/canada/montreal-is-falling-down, (accessed June 2019).

LeClair, A. October 19, 2016. "New Overpass Leading to the Champlain Bridge Demolished, Will Be Rebuilt," *Global News.* https://globalnews.ca/news/3013692/new-overpass-leading-to-champlain-bridge-demolished-will-be-rebuilt/.

Perreaux, L. November 29, 2013. "Champlain Bridge Is Falling Down: Montreal Pays for Past Penny Pinching," *The Globe and Mail.* https://

www.theglobeandmail.com/news/national/champlain-bridge-is-falling-down-montreal-pays-for-past-penny-pinching/article15699180, (accessed June 2019).

Rewards and Employee Benefits Association. January 24, 2018. "Research: Attitudes to Employee Share Ownership." https://reba.global/reports/research-attitudes-to-employee-share-ownership, (accessed June 2019).

Chapter 5

Bainbridge, S.M. 2002. "Why a Board? Group Decision Making in Corporate Governance." *Vanderbilt Law Review* 55, no. 1, pp. 1-55.

Bois, J. December 2, 2015. "A Eulogy for RadioShack, the Panicked and Half-Deal Retail Store," *SBNation*. https//www.sbnation.com/2014/11/26/7281129/radioshack-eulogy-stories, (accessed August 2019).

Cox, C. October, 2010. "How to Be the Perfect Board Member," *dmagazine*. https://www.dmagazine.com/publications/d-ceo/2010/october/how-to/be-perfect-corporate-board-member, (accessed August 2019).

Dada, G.A. July 7, 2016. "RadioShack Strategy: A Lesson for Business Leaders," *Adaptive Marketer*. https://theadaptivemarketer.com/2016/07/07/radioshack-strategy-a-lesson, (accessed August 2019).

Gevurtz, F.A. May 15, 2004. "The Historical and Political Origins of the Corporate Board of Directors," *Social Science Research Network*. https://papers.ssrn.com/so13/papers.cfm?abstract_id=546296, (accessed August 2019).

Hamilton, A. August, 1791. "Prospectus of the Society for Establishing Useful Manufactures," *Founders Online*. https://founders.archives.gov/documents/Hamilton/01-09-02-0114, (accessed September 1, 2019).

Larcker, D., and B. Tayan. n.d. "Board of Directors Duties and Liabilities," *Stanford University Corporate Governance Research Initiative*. https://www.gsb.stanford.edu/faculty-research/publications/board-directors-duties-liabilities, (accessed September 2019).

Law Insider. May 23, 2011. "RadioShack Corporation Bylaws Amended and Restated as of May 19, 2011," *Law Insider.* https://www.lawinsider.com/contracts/28DqrUeEPohxiIJENGkjSN/radioshack-corp/0/2011-05-23, (accessed September 2019).

Moore, R. December 5, 2014. "With No Presumption of Prudence, RadioShack Faces New Lawsuit," *Compliance.* https://www.plansponsor.com/with-no-presumption-of-prudence-radioshack-faces-new-lawsuit, (accessed September 2019).

Silverman, D. July 23, 2016. "Dynamic Capability in Action: Why RadioShack Failed." *Slide Share.* https://www.slideshare.net/DavidASilverman/dynamic-capability-in-action-why-radioshack-failed-64298888, (accessed September 2019).

Sonnenfeld, J.A. September, 2002. "What Makes Great Boards Great." *Harvard Business Review.* https://hbr.org/2002/09/what-makes-great-boards-great, (accessed September 2019).

U.S. Securities and Exchange Commission. March 4, 2014. "RadioShack." https://www.sec.gov/Archives/edgar/data/96289/000009628914000005/form10k123113.htm, (accessed September 2019).

Wolf, A. September, 12015. "RadioShack Creditors on the Warpath," *Twice.* https://www.twice.com/retailing/radioshack-creditors-warpath-584, (accessed September 2019).

Chapter 6

Jackson, W.S., S. Druck, and S. Albury. 2016. "Delivering the Future 2016: How the G20's Postal Services Are Meeting the Challenges of the 21st Century," *Oxford Strategic Consulting.* http://www.oxfordstrategicconsulting.com/wp-content/uploads/2017/09/Delivering-the-Future-of-the-Postal-Service-in-the-G20-Final-Report-March-2017.pdf, (accessed September 2019).

Moreno, K. March 18, 2014. "4 Steps to a Successful Business Transformation," *Forbes Magazine.* https://www.forbes.com/sites/forbesinsights/2014/03/18/4-steps-to-a-successful-business-transformation/#24eb29521807, (accessed September 2019).

U.S. General Accounting Office. 2002. *U.S. Postal Service: Deteriorating Financial Outlook Increases Need for Transformation.* GAO-020355. Washington, DC: U.S. GAO. https://www.gao.gov/assets/240/233844.pdf

U.S. Postal Service. September 30, 2001. "Outline for Discussion: Concepts for Postal Transformation," *U.S. Postal Service.* https://about.usps.com/strategic-planning/outbody.pdf, (accessed September 2019).

U.S. Postal Service. April, 2002. "Transformation Plan," *U.S. Postal Service.* https://about.usps.com/strategic-planning/2002transformationplan.pdf

U.S. Postal Service. September, 2005. "Strategic Transformation Plan 2006–2010," *U.S. Postal Service.* https://about.usps.com/strategic-planning/stp2006-2010/stp05r.pdf, (accessed September 2019).

U.S. Postal Service. n.d. "Future Ready: Five Year Strategic Plan (USPS), 2017-2021," *U.S. Post Service.* https://about.usps.com/strategic-planning/five-year-strategic-plan-2017-2021.pdf, (accessed September 2019).

About the Authors

Daniel L. Plung is recognized for developing innovative business practices. He has 40+ years of experience working for a variety of Fortune 500 corporations. He has had assignments on multibillion-dollar projects in both the United States and the United Kingdom, with leadership responsibility for all project phases from proposal development through contract closeout. Trained in both LEAN and Six Sigma, much of his career has focused on process improvement and project transformations. In addition to applying his skills in engineering, technology, and nuclear-related service industries, Dr. Plung has also supported successful transformation efforts undertaken by nonprofit agencies and government programs.

A graduate of the Bronx HS of Science, the City College of New York, and Idaho State University, he has served on the Washington State Board of Education; on the faculty of Idaho State University, University of South Carolina, and Washington State University; and on an advisory board for New Mexico Tech. In addition to keynoting professional conferences, Dr. Plung is the author of more than 50 publications, including two anthologies and one college textbook on professional communication.

Connie J. Krull has had a succession of assignments focused on strategic management and strategic planning—with extensive accolades for limiting risk, developing effective long-term business strategies, and optimizing internal operations. She has a demonstrated history of leadership, with managerial assignments in contract management, project operations, facility management, supply chain management, warehouse services, procurement, business services, and strategic planning and implementation.

Ms. Krull's breadth of experience in administrative, business, and technical assignments provides a broad foundation for designing and implementing integrated and innovative solutions to challenges faced by industries undergoing transformation.

Ms. Krull holds a bachelor of science in business, with an emphasis on project management, and a master's degree in business administration (MBA).

She has more than 25 years of experience supporting and managing infrastructure, and operations and maintenance activities. During her career, she has worked on numerous projects with responsibility for expanding services in support of new requirements, upgrading existing programs, and developing a systematic approach to fostering an organization's preparation and ability to move forward aggressively during times of change. Ms. Krull is also currently serving as vice chair of the Board of Trustees for a not-for-profit utilities company, with responsibilities including long-term planning and development of multiyear investment strategies.

Index

www.ingramcontent.com/pod-product-compliance
Lightning Source LLC
Chambersburg PA
CBHW061309220326
41599CB00026B/4799